WILLIAM MARSHAL

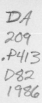

WILLIAM MARShAL

The FLOWER
OF
ChivALRy

GEORGES DUBY

TRANSLATED FROM THE FRENCH

BY RICHARD HOWARD

PANTHEON BOOKS · NEW YORK

Library of Congress Cataloging-in-Publication Data

Duby, Georges.
  William Marshal: the flower of chivalry.

  Translation of: Guillaume le Maréchal.
  Bibliography: p.
  1. Pembroke, William Marshal, Earl of, 1144?–1219. 2. Regents—Great Britain —Biography. 3. Knights and knighthood—Great Britain—History. 4. Chivalry. 5. Great Britain—History—Angevin period, 1154–1216. I. Title.
DA209.P413D82   1986   942.03′4′0924 [B]   85-42837
ISBN 0-394-54309-2

Book design by Jennifer Dossin

Manufactured in the United States of America

First American Edition

WILLIAM MARSHAL

I

𝒯HE EARL can bear no more. The burden is too great for him now. Three years ago, when he was urged to assume the regency, when he reluctantly agreed, becoming "master and guardian" of the boy king and of the whole realm of England, he had said and said again, "I am too old, too weak, too out of joint." Over eighty, he had claimed, exaggerating a little, not really knowing how old he was. Who knew such things in those days? Other dates in life mattered more than when you were born. You could forget that one. And grand old men were so rare that you made them out even older than they reckoned themselves. Moreover, we ourselves don't know just when William Marshal was born. The historians have worked it out; they propose around 1145. No more specific than that. His birth is too low for the archives to be much help. Whereas in the year we are now speaking of—1219—fortune has raised him so high that we can follow, almost day by day, his final deeds, his last exploits.

Robust he had remained—a very long time. He had been seen fighting the French at Lincoln on May 20, 1217, like a youth among his peers. Three months later, his men had still had to hold him back—did he not try to join the sailors at Sandwich and board the French fleet? But all of a sudden, on Candlemas of 1219, he gave way. He had felt it coming, and for some time, without speaking of it, had been preparing for his last campaign. He returned for a spell to Marlborough Castle, probably his own birthplace. On March 7 he is at

Westminster, and from there, "riding down his pain," he reaches the Tower of London, as if to huddle behind the walls of the old royal stronghold. He takes to his bed. It is the beginning of Lent. What better time to suffer, to accept your suffering, to endure it in remission of your sins, and to purify yourself slowly, calmly, before the great journey? His countess is beside him, as always. When he weakens, when the doctors admit they can do no more, William Marshal summons those who have accompanied him ever since he quit private life. Naturally. Necessarily. Had he ever been alone? Who is ever alone at the beginning of the thirteenth century but the mad, the possessed—marginal figures who are hunted down? An orderly world requires that each man remain swathed in a fabric of solidarities, of friendships, in a *corps*. William summons those who constitute the body of which he is the head. A group of men. His men: the knights of his house; and then his eldest son. He requires this numerous retinue for the great ceremony about to begin—that of a princely death. Once everyone is there to form the cortege, he gives orders that he be borne away. At home, he says, he will suffer more comfortably. Best to die in your own house. Bear him to Caversham, to his own manor. He owns many, but this is the one he chooses, for in the country of his birth it is the closest, the most accessible. Mounting a horse is out of the question now; the Thames will bear him to it. So on March 16, William, Earl of Pembroke, is "arrayed" by his people in one boat, his wife following in another, and gently, without great exertion, the little convoy is rowed upstream.

On arrival, his first concern is to free himself from the burden that weighs upon him. The man whose end is approaching must gradually rid himself of everything, and before all else, the honors of this world. First act, first rite of renunciation. Ostentatious, like all the acts to follow, for good deaths in this age are festivities, they are *performed* as on a stage before many spectators, many auditors attentive to every gesture, to every word, eager for the dying man to show what he is worth, to speak, to act according to his rank, to bequeath a final example of virtue to those who will follow. Each man, in this fashion, as he leaves the world is obliged, one last time, to shore up that morality which holds the social body together, which allows each generation to succeed the next in the order pleasing to God. And we, who no longer know the meaning of a *sumptuous death,* we who hide death away, who hush it up, who get rid of it as fast as we can—an embarrassing business—we for whom a good death must be swift, discreet, solitary, let us take advantage of the fact that the greatness to which the earl has acceded puts him, for our eyes, in an exceptionally brilliant light. Let us follow step by step, in all the details of its unfolding, the ritual of death in the old style, which was not an evasion, a furtive exit, but a slow, orderly approach, a careful prelude, a solemn transfer from one condition to another, to a higher state, a transition as public as the weddings of the period, as majestic as the entrances of kings into their fine cities. The death that we have lost and that, it may well be, we miss.

The office that still invests the dying earl is of such weight that every man of consequence within the state must see with his own eyes how William leaves it, and what he will do with it. The king, of course, and the papal legate as well—since Rome, in this first quarter of the thirteenth century, regards the kingdom of England as under its protection and control —the capital justiciar, but also all the higher barony. A great crowd, which has gathered for this purpose and cannot be contained within the manor house of Caversham. It encamps across the river, at Reading, in the great royal monastery and its grounds. William cannot leave his bed. Therefore, the great men of the realm cross the river to stand at his bedside. On April 8 or 9 they come into his chamber, accompanying a boy of twelve, young King Henry. It is this child whom the earl begins by lecturing from his bed, apologizing that he can serve him no longer and elaborating that sermon which, ac-

5

cording to the rules, all fathers must make on their deathbed to their eldest son and heir. William admonishes the boy, commends him to a proper life, and prays God, he says, to bring him to immediate ruin should he become, by some mischance, a traitor in the unfortunate fashion of some of his forebears. And the entire company replies, Amen. Then the earl dismisses them. He is not ready. He needs the night to determine who shall succeed him as guardian. He decides to pass over the bishop of Winchester, an ambitious man who just now had held the boy fast, presuming he had control over him because in 1216 the earl had entrusted to his "vice-regency" a child too young to accompany the regent's incessant expeditions; and now the bishop was trying to get the boy into his power. William needs time to think, to seek advice—from his son, his people, his intimates. In his own family, in private, he makes up his mind: there are too many rivalries in the country today. Were he to entrust Henry, third of the name, to one faction, others would thereby be roused, and once again there would be war. Of all the barons, William alone had the necessary authority. Who could take his place? God, quite simply. God and the pope. To them, therefore, he will entrust the king—that is, to the legate who stands for the former, and in England for the latter.

This he does the following day, still in bed but propped up as high as he can bear, summoning the king, first taking the royal hand in his, then joining the legate's with it, lastly commanding his own son to cross the Thames to Reading where the whole court remains, so that in his own name before all, and repudiating the bishop of Winchester who maintains his claim and still hugs the crowned child, he will repeat the gesture of joined hands that has just been made—that very simple, very visible sign, the rite of renunciation and of investiture whereby the transfer of power is effected.

Whereby, too, he is relieved. That evening, he speaks once again, saying the words that must be said. Here they are, at least as they were recalled in the household after his death, words considered worthy of his fame: "I am already delivered. Yet it is well that I go further, that I take care for my soul, since my body is in peril, that in your hearing I complete my release from all earthly things, in order to think only of celestial ones." Such indeed is the prescribed order: one's body must be gradually discarded, a useless castoff, like all that relates to the flesh, to the world. The dying man must do his utmost, at the last, to lighten himself, to ascend the sooner and the higher. It is this detachment, indeed this ascent, that is in question. A man who dies must, at the moment of his *exitus*, present himself naked as he emerged from his mother's womb. For a rebirth—to a new life, and a better one. And this second birth, this death, matters much more than the first one. Its date, in each biography of the earl's contemporaries, was of all dates the one most solidly fixed in men's memories.

The relinquishment continues. Now that the earl has surrendered public office, it is expected that he will open his hand wider and release what it still holds, his private possessions, all his lands. The spectators, the auditors await the second scene of this first act, the scene of the distribution, of the division of the inheritance. Let the dead man "seize" the living, which is to say, let him put in "seizin"—in possession —those among the living who are entitled to what he has till now possessed, having himself received it from others. No gestures this time. Those present do not watch an object passing from hand to hand. They listen. They hoard words in memory in order to repeat them later, if need be. William, loud and clear, speaks his will. As a matter of fact, he has very little choice. Everyone knows more or less what must come to each according to custom, that unwritten law as constraining as the most rigid codes. The rule, moreover, is simple: there is only one "natural" heir, the man in whom the deceased will survive, who bears the same name as he, William Marshal the younger, his eldest son. By this claim, because he is a boy and because he is the firstborn he will be entitled to everything. For it is incumbent upon him to take beside his mother the place his father will soon cease to fill, to protect her against others and against herself, to manage her estate and her possessions. To his wife, indeed, who is also listening, old William leaves nothing. Nor can he. All that he owned, or very nearly, and of which he is stripping himself now, belongs to this woman, comes from her ancestors, and he has never held any of it save in her name, *"de son chef."* These vast estates the eldest son as the rightful heir will hold in turn till she dies.

Yet he has four brothers and five sisters. We are not aware that the other boys are present. It is certain, in any case, that the oldest of these, Richard, is far away in France at the time, and in the other camp, at the court of Philip Augustus. Those present learn that this second son is to receive a handsome share of the succession, the seigneury of Longueville in Normandy, which not long since his father, William, had acquired from the Capetian. Such a legacy is a concession, even a favor, but one it is good to grant, if it will keep Richard quiet, so that unlike so many disinherited second sons he will not envy and torment and execrate his older brother. Gilbert, the third boy, is settled in the Church, and well settled, having already paid for his (lucrative) place there: he needs nothing and has nothing. To Walter, the fourth son, a manor is bequeathed, but a small one, not taken from the ancestral patrimony; such a legacy does not cut into the landed basis of power and prestige which each generation in this age is charged to transmit intact, if not augmented, to the next. Marshal has just bought this holding; he is free to dispose of it as he wishes.

There remains Anselm, the lastborn boy, still very young. For him there is no land left. William speaks: "Very dear to me is this last son. But he must live long enough to become a knight, he must ride errant till he win honor; then he will find someone who will cherish him and do him great honor, more than any other." By which we may understand: in his youngest son, who is the nearest to his heart if not to his flesh, since he may be the only one who has not yet left the house for his apprenticeship, the dying man sees the one whose destiny might come to resemble his own, who might raise himself heroically, just as William did, by his own powers, starting from nothing, to glory. His decision is one of trust and even, who knows, tenderness. Yet his old friend, John d'Erley, intervenes, remonstrating: "You cannot do this thing; give him of what you have [that is, some money], at least enough to shoe his horse. Else it will be ill done." William acquiesces; yet he assigns no land to the boy; he settles on Anselm an annual income of 140 pounds. A pension that can be terminated if the boy turns out badly. The income is attractive: with such a sum one could at the time buy at least three good war-horses.

And the daughters? Thanks be to God, four are married, and well married at that, to some of the richest barons of England. They are already provided for, since their father, before their weddings, has given them dowries; they have nothing more to expect. But the youngest girl, Jeanne, remains unmarried, and the dying man is concerned about her: "In my lifetime, I have given her nothing. Alas, my soul will find no peace in that." It is indeed the father's preoccupation: to avoid leaving unmarried orphans behind him. "Desolate," which means alone. Without a man whose responsibility it would be to find her a husband, agreeing to meet the price such things cost. For it is not customary, in the period, to take for a wife a woman who has nothing, and even quite commonly, in the great world, men form unions with those richer than themselves. Girls without sustenance, without possessions, will find few takers, and if their weddings are too long delayed, such girls run a great risk, as William Marshal well knows, of "going to their shame." Deprived of masculine guidance, rare are those who are not dissolute. He can count on his eldest son, of course, whose duty is to marry off his sister as soon as possible. To facilitate his task, to attract eventual clients, William does what he has the power to do and which everyone considers adequate: he settles on Jeanne another, smaller income of thirty pounds; moreover, he takes from his treasury, where he can draw freely, a great heap of money, two hundred marks, for the trousseau.

S UCH testamentary arrangements were pursued, at the beginning of the thirteenth century, by all of the aristocracy of England and northern France. Dowries excluding daughters from succession, rights of primogeniture, diminished by a few small gifts in favor of younger sons in order not to destroy fraternal accord—these customs assured the stability of patrimonies and consequently of the foundations on which the superiority of the ruling class was firmly established, in a hierarchy of earthly conditions regarded as conforming to divine intentions. Custom in this age supports the order of the world. It is virtually sacred, and not to be infringed. Yet it is proper that the head of the house, at the moment of yielding up his soul, himself make clear his wishes, his choices. Hence words first, and in public. They will suffice. Yet care is taken to entrust them to writing in order that all be well ascertained. No man of law here at the time. The will is written in the household by those of the servitors who can write. William orders that his privy seal be set to it, but also that his wife and eldest son set theirs as well, they being, with him, the sole possessors of all property; what he has bequeathed is taken from their share. Yet even this is not enough. He orders that the parchment be taken to the archbishop of Canterbury, to the legate, to the bishops of Salisbury and Winchester, so that they too may seal it and fulminate the ritual excommunications against possible violators. Armed with these guarantees, the document is shut away in a strongbox. It is unlikely that there will

10

ever be a need to read it. But the solid words it contains as though in a reliquary now belong to the family treasure.

The dying man, taking his time, is henceforth rid of the heaviest burdens. Yet he remains attached to earth by his body. According to the rules, the concern for the body intervenes at this point of the ceremony, third phase of the gradual denudation. Marshal turns to John d'Erley: "Go and ask for the two silken cloths, which I left with Stephen d'Evreux." When he holds these in his hands, he addresses himself to Henry Fitzgerald, who is second in friendship among his most loyal companions, though Henry, no more than John d'Erley, is neither William's relative nor his equal; they are beneath him, he rules them, and for this, nothing prevents him from loving them greatly. We feel that he loves them more than he loves his children, that he relies on them more, that they are his true intimates. "A little worn? Let them be unfolded." Then the fine stuff is clearly seen, offered to the admiration of the company, the son and all the household knights. "My lords, consider. These cloths I have had for thirty years; when I returned from across the sea, I brought them with me in order to make such use of them as now I shall. Let them be spread out upon my body when I am laid in earth." "But where?" In the mouth of the heir who must direct the funeral arrangements, the grave and urgent question that is echoed by all those present. For the dying man must designate his last resting place, must express at this very moment his desire as to the flesh he is leaving. "My fair son, when I was over the sea, I gave my body to the Temple in order to rest there upon my death." And then, turning to John d'Erley, "You will spread them upon me, once I am dead. You will cover the bier with them. And if it should be bad weather, buy then some good heavy gray cloth of whatever kind, place it on top so that the silk not be spoiled, and leave it to the brothers of the Temple once I am buried, that they may do with it as they please."

11

S O LONG as it was only a matter of the inheritance, the decisive step did not yet seem to have been taken: had not someone, twenty years ago, heard William Marshal already dictate his last will and testament? But now he has spoken of burial, referred to the funeral procession. We find that this time the die is cast, that he is readying himself to depart this life. Therefore, it is at this moment that the demonstrations of mourning are initiated. Now come the tears. The household sets itself to weeping, tenderly, grievously. All the men—the son, the knights, the squires, even the humblest servants. Of the women's tears, not much is made. But the appearance of men's tears marks the threshold of the final act. William the Younger then leaves the death chamber, calling in whoever among the knighthood is not yet present. The time has come to organize the vigils. The dying man has chosen his sepulcher, the place where he desires his body to lie until the resurrection. This body, by his words, he has entrusted to those who will carry out his wishes. It no longer altogether belongs to him. Moreover, he no longer holds on to his soul so securely. Consequently, he must be more closely guarded by those who are now responsible for him. This corporeal envelope henceforth drifts toward death: who knows what impulses will disturb it now, altering its color and its odor? It is a source of anxiety. This tragically disintegrating person must no longer be left without surveillance, abandoned to solitude. Let a watch be kept at all times over this body. Three knights. They will be relayed, night and day. Accompanied by John d'Erley and Thomas Basset, William the heir will take the most perilous watch: he will keep vigil by night, during those uncertain hours when the Demon prowls.

At this moment, room is first made for religious preoccupations. What we learn from William Marshal's last moments is, for historians, very precious. The narrative on which I am relying explicitly reveals the way in which men of his time and social station experienced their Christianity. It allows us to rectify two fallacious kinds of evidence: first, that of hagiographic literature which paints every knight as a little Saint Alexis, a little Saint Maurice, steeped in docile devotion; then the evidence of the tales of chivalry, the literature opposing clerical ideology and, conversely, overemphasizing the secular realm. The true piety that appears here is a tranquil trust in God, resorting to priests only in moderation. And it is in the institutional context best suited to the spirit of knighthood, the Order of the Templars, that the concern for religious matters is first manifested here.

During the pilgrimage when he spent several months in the Holy Land in 1185, William Marshal could have seen these warrior-monks in action and in their full power. He observed them imperiling their own bodies in the struggle for Christ while remaining strictly obedient to monastic discipline, submitting without hesitation or resistance, possessing nothing of their own, never touching women, denying themselves any form of boastful speech, gambling, and any useless embellishments. As a connoisseur, he admired how joyously, how effectively they outstripped all others in battle. He realized that in their persons they combined the merits of the two ruling categories of human society, the religious order and the chivalric order, and that these men thereby stood, judging from all appearances, in the forefront of those who will reach paradise. Hence he had determined, years ago, to become one of their company. Yet hesitating to leave the world so soon, he had simply, as he said just now, "given." The procedure was a common one at the time. At the end of the twelfth century, many gentlemen (whose grandparents, long before, on their deathbeds had asked to be robed in the sackcloth of the Benedictines) thus joined the flourishing congregation of the Templars, committing themselves, yet not consenting to take the habit until later, at the right moment, which is to say at the onset of death, thereby enjoying, having fulfilled their pledge *in extremis*, all the favors promised to members of the company in good standing. For William, the hour has come, he knows: "he has not the talent to wait any longer."

Aimery de Sainte-Maure, from Touraine, a friend of the Plantagenet kings, master of the Temple in London, is informed. He knows that the earl wants to be buried in the house he rules. He arrives while there is still time to undertake the official reception of the dying man. It must take place, formally, before all his people, since he will be separating himself from them in order to make his way into another family. The wives of his relatives too must be present. The countess and her daughters are summoned. The rite is once again one of passage. The transfer from knighthood to the "new" knighthood, as Saint Bernard called it, the renewed knighthood, that of the "new men" who have determined to become more nearly perfect. It may well be that this rite, at the beginning of the thirteenth century, seems somewhat antiquated. Forms of devotion are evolving very rapidly at this time. Monasticism is in decline, especially the military variety. Many fewer are the young men who still choose to become Templars, to join these knights whose failure overseas is patent, who, it is murmured, are not so pure, who are overly concerned with handling money, and who—it is already imagined—abandon themselves to curious practices in the secrecy of their commanderies. But William is a survivor. It is not a common thing to live so long as he in this milieu, among these horsemen who eat like wolves, drink like hounds, and who are bedridden by strokes when they are not brutally mowed down by the exercise of their profession. Till now, for example, none of the kings of France has lived past his fiftieth year. One must be a bishop or a Cluniac monk to reach that age with ease. The donation of himself which the earl has made is thirty years old. Would he make the same pledge today, he who has not belonged for a long time to the minor orders of knighthood, but to the great world in which fashion is eagerly followed in matters of piety as in all others? He figures here as the rare witness of bygone attitudes. He is aware of this and says as much: "Hear me: it was a very long time ago that I gave myself to the Temple; now I keep my promise."

Therefore, let someone take out of his wardrobe the white cloak with the red cross; he has had it embroidered a year ago, and only Geoffrey the Templar shares with him the knowledge of its existence. He is lying in his bed and cannot be dressed in the cloak. This emblem of his new condition must be spread before him. To change orders is to change clothes. Above all, it is to change one's way of living, to contract different obligations. Henceforth William is a Templar. Forever. The Templars are monks. They are forbidden to approach women. Hence William will no longer approach his wife. At this moment, then, he takes leave of the woman who for twenty years has made one flesh with his: "Sweet friend, embrace me here, you will never do as much again." He stretches up as high as he can from the bed, so that in a final kiss their mouths may meet. There are tears on both sides. The countess and her daughters are taken away, swooning, while Master Aimery speaks in his turn, and before those present utters the appropriate sentences.

AND NOW there is nothing more to do but let time have its way, to wait, to follow the progress of this lingering agony. It lasts for two months, and with it the great spectacle I am describing, whose tempo becomes extraordinarily deliberate. The public might weary of it—it perseveres. The death chamber never empties. In order to see how the earl is dying, people elbow their way beside the eldest son, almost always seated—patient, faithful, playing his part perfectly—beside the deathbed. Such a crowd, such assiduity, testify to the prestige of the man who is slowly taking his leave. The whole household therefore rejoices, devotes itself to prolonging this wondrous longevity by every means, for it constitutes the glory of the family. William is no longer hungry. Yet he must eat, in order that nature persist "performing her labors within him." He is continually pestered, stuffed, bread being crumbled into the mushrooms he still is willing to swallow, without suspecting the ruse. Everyone is anxious, but to no purpose: life clings to this great carcass. At times, in fact, impulses of vitality course through him. One day, the dying man questions John d'Erley; "Can I tell you a great piece of news?" "Yes, sire, if the saying of it does not tire you." "I know not whence it may come, but it has been three years or more since I have known so strong a craving to sing as I have felt these last three days. Now I ask myself, can God see such a thing with favoring eyes?" "Proceed, sire, sing. Nature is taking strength within you. It would be a great boon as well if you were to take some thought for eating." "Speak no more. Singing would do me no good. My people here would regard me as a man gone mad, and would believe I had lost my wits."

Indeed, it is quite seemly to sing at weddings or after tournaments. But a near-dead man who sings, if he does not sing the psalms of penitence in company with the priests: scandal. Then Henry Fitzgerald, his other court friend, counsels, "Summon your daughters, they will sing for you. You shall see, their singing will comfort you." The daughters are brought in. William orders the eldest, Maheut "Bigotte," wife of Hugh Bigot, future earl of Norfolk, to sing first. She obeys; she forces herself; but of course her heart isn't in it. Then comes the turn of the youngest, the unwed and therefore most pitied of her sisters. Her voice cracks, she loses her part. Her father, supposing this a result of timidity, reproves her: "Have no shame." And then shows her how to proceed, speaking the words, "one sound at a time."

That night is the last time he saw his five daughters, and when he had sent them back to their mother, he seemed, though usually so much the master of his feelings, greatly

16

moved. Forcing back his distress, he quickly moves on to serious matters, describes in detail to his son the arrangements of his funeral ceremonies: let William the Younger be closest to him when he enters—when *his body* enters London. He also wants the poor to be thought of. He is certain they will gather round the cortege in great numbers. A service of such opulence is not often seen. Of these poor folk, he determines that at least a hundred will be fed, given drink, and clothed after the ceremony.

Throughout the day he is solicited. Sometimes to take food —no respite: he must eat—sometimes to take thought for his soul—no respite: he must give. For to give is to wash away his sins. Since the lands he held in his wife's name are now out of his hands, abandoned to the heir, he must for his salvation rid himself of what he still possesses, that is, his treasure, those very precious liquid assets that belong to himself alone, to which he is utterly entitled, which everyone knows to be heaped in his bedchamber in the locked hiding place bulging with robes, ornaments, moneys, rings. The moment has come to disperse this hoard whose weight risks dragging his soul down to hell. That is what the churchmen keep telling him. For they are here now, increasingly numerous, drawn by this windfall. Among them the abbot of Nutley, who has just returned from the chapter general of his order, that of Arrouaise; he has heard that the earl is in the last extremity; the canons have decided to receive him as a fellow-member, to share with him the favors profusely stored up by the prayers and good works of this charitable order; the abbot has come specifically to bring this good news; he furnishes his proofs, shows the sealed letters with which he has been provided. Let the dying man be reassured. And generous. And so he is. All those around him urge him on.

Above all, let nothing be forgotten. Let him empty out all his strongboxes and bins. Those most intent upon rousing his largesse are, of course, his closest friends, those who

17

truly love him. Henry Fitzgerald and the clerk of his house, Philip. These men ask nothing for themselves. Disinterested, they are concerned only to save a suffering soul by distributing gifts among Christ's poor, first of all among those who not only possess nothing but who sanctify their poverty by mortifications, by renunciations, and whose prayers are thereby most effective, most capable of deflecting the wrath of God. But the dying man can also save his soul, and perhaps first of all, by settling his debts, by making amends for the wrongs he has done. As a matter of fact, to make confession, to acknowledge his sins, is not enough. He is expressly commanded to recall to mind the names of all those he has harmed throughout his existence, in order to compensate them. He must restore all he has taken, the plunder of his greed, if he hopes that his torments will be spared in the life to come. William's friends repeat this to him tirelessly to the point of importunity. Vexed, he does not restrain his harsh words. The moment is one of great seriousness. He risks a great deal—he risks everything. Yet he does not hesitate to say aloud just what he is thinking, which may seem incongruous. He too knows the import of what he says. Of him is expected, as of all dying men whose words are listened to attentively, the teaching of a final lesson, setting forth true morality.

Such a morality is not that of the priests, which profits them much. Nor that of the sanctimonious. It is the morality of knighthood, of chivalry. Now—and this is what matters to us—historians are much less well informed about this morality than the other kinds. So let us listen to him, as the crowd around his bed listened to him at this moment, carefully registering for lineal posterity the pronouncement he then had the courage to make: "The churchmen work against us; they shave us too close. I have captured in my lifetime at least five hundred knights whose arms, horses, and caparisons I have taken for my own. If the kingdom of God is denied me for this reason, I can do nothing about it. Would you have me yield it all up again? For God I can do no more than to offer him myself, repenting of all the sins I have committed. If the priests and clerks would not have me cast out, rejected, excluded, they must leave me in peace. Either their argument is false, or else no man can be saved."

And later, in the very last moments, when he is reminded that his wardrobe is still full: he cannot take with him all the garments of scarlet and miniver it contains, and eighty adorned with precious furs, all fresh and new; let him make haste to have them sold, for with the money, judiciously distributed among the religious communities, he will buy prayers, which is to say, the instruments of his redemption. Whereupon William becomes angry outright: "Say no more, wretches. I have had enough of your advice. Soon it will be Pentecost, the season when the knights of my house are to receive their new gowns. This I know, and never again shall I be able to bestow such things upon them. Yet it is now that you seek to prevent me. Approach, John d'Erley. By that faith you owe to God and to me, I order you to make on my behalf the distribution of all these gowns. And if there are not enough here for everyone of my house, send yet again to London to buy what is lacking. Let none of my people have to complain of me."

A good seigneur first of all makes every effort not to transgress the precepts of domestic morality, which oblige him to deal generously with those of his household, nor those of social morality, which prescribe that the knights, whose order is at the apex of the hierarchy, be clad more richly than others. A good seigneur thinks first of his own people, of those he keeps in his house and who owe all to his generosity. A good seigneur, such as the holy King Louis a few years later, also knows the essential value of the body's ornaments in a culture of ostentation and display, in a society where a man is judged by what he wears upon his back. He knows he must be dressed well in order to be loved, feared, served. The earl is a good seigneur. It is in this aspect that he wishes to abide in the memory of his people, in the plenitude of the virtues suited to his state, which are of a sumptuous generosity. Thus the night was spent in the distribution of squirrel, of silk, of sable. All the knights put on the fairest of what their master's body had worn. The little that remained, the least good, was abandoned to the poor. In each of the men who thus sported his finery, one might imagine that the dying man was restored to life. On the Sunday before Ascension, William was thus ceremoniously stripped of his gowns. He no longer possessed anything but his shroud. He was ready for the journey.

He had already charged his son to say farewell on his behalf to all those who had served him and who were not present to forgive him for anything he might have said or done. The next day, William the Younger, kneeling, begged his father, for the love of Christ, to eat something: "We are certain it will do you good." "Then for that," he acquiesced, "I shall eat as much as I can." Out of kindness. He sat up, supported by a knight. When the cloth was laid, he summoned John d'Erley. "Do you see what I see?" "My lord, I do not know what that might be." "By my soul, I see two men in white; one is beside me on the right, the other on the left; nowhere have I seen men so fine." "My lord, thus there comes to you a company that will lead you in the true way." Then the earl began repeating: "Blessed be the Lord our God, who hitherto has granted me His grace." As for John d'Erley, he never forgave himself for not asking who these two persons were, so dazzling in their whiteness. Angels? Saints? Venerable ancestors returning to earth? Whatever they were, their presence proved that the gates of the other world were opening. These harbingers came to greet the earl, to provide him an escort. The sign was clear: he was soon to pass on.

On Tuesday, May 14, 1219, at the hour of noon, his son returns, with the others. He finds the earl turned to face the wall, resting in peace. They believe him to be asleep, and the young earl gives orders that silence be maintained and that the company withdraw. "Who is there?" "It is I, John d'Erley." "John, is that you?" "Yes, sire." "I cannot sleep." "How could you sleep, it is fifteen days since you have eaten anything at all." William Marshal turns over, stretches his limbs. The death pains begin to be felt. "John, make haste, open wide the doors and windows. Call my son here, the countess, the knights. I am dying now, I cannot wait any longer, I wish to take my leave of them." John rushes to open all the doors and windows, then returns and embraces the earl who, lying face down, swoons and closes his eyes. He comes to. "John. Did I faint?" "Yes, sire." "I've never seen you look so helpless. Why haven't you rinsed my face with rose-water, so that I may speak properly to these good people? For I have not much longer to do so." Reinvigorated by the scented water, and everyone being present, he can utter the last words. He pronounces his death very simply: "I am dying. I commend you to God. I can no longer remain with you. I cannot defend myself from death." He then enters into the silence.

John d'Erley moves back, giving way to the one who must now take his place. The son sits down. Weeping very gently, which is to say, in his heart and not to display his tears, he puts his arms about his father, who nestles there like a child. The priests, since their share had been given, since the dying man had nothing more he could give, had discreetly withdrawn. Now they press forward, the abbot of Nutley, accompanied by his canons, the abbot of Reading, accompanied by his monks and bearing on the legate's behalf the pontifical absolution granting a plenary indulgence. Did the earl even need such a thing? Since the beginning of his illness, he had confessed each week. In great pomp, which never spoils anything, the two abbots absolve him one last time. Some claim that they saw him nod and even raise his hand, as if to cross himself, worshipping the cross placed in front of his eyes. He gives up the ghost. There is no indication that he received the viaticum.

$\mathcal{T}$ HIS IS not the end of the spectacle: the soul is departed, but the body remains. Exposed to all eyes in the center of the stage, it still has its role to play. In front of it, while it abides in its private dwelling, before it crosses the manor threshold to its last resting place, the Temple in London, the abbot of Reading returns to celebrate the mass in the domestic chapel for a fee of one hundred sous granted him by William the Younger and his mother. The cortege forms and begins to move. Two halts have been arranged. At each of them, the earl's body spends the night in a church, a safe place: first the abbey church of Reading, then that of Staines. In these places it is joined by all the earls of the region, the earl of Surrey, the earl of Essex, the earl of Oxford; from farther away have come the earl of Gloucester, Gilbert de Clare, the husband of William's second daughter. These noble persons, surrounded by their retinues, form a brilliant guard of honor. By thus favoring the luster of the funeral procession, God further proved to the earl the kindness he had shown him all his life. Entering London, the body was greeted by the archbishop of Canterbury, the primate of England. The vigil, in the candlelit church of the Temple, echoing with holy music, was splendid. Everything was so fine, so well done, so glorious that those present, their hearts filled, forgot their grief. They thanked heaven for the honor it deigned to show the deceased. The next morning, preparations were made for laying the body in earth before the great cross, next to the tomb of Master Aimery, who had given up the ghost while awaiting the earl's death.

At the end of the funeral ceremonies, laid out on the bier before the open grave, the earl's mute body spoke still. It instructed all those present, a countless horde, as had been expected. Before their eyes, this body offered itself as the image of what each of them would one day be. Inevitably. "Mirror"—that is how the archbishop defined it in the sermon he delivered for the edification of the crowd. "See, my lords, what the world comes to. Each man, when he has reached this point, no longer signifies anything but this: he is no more than a lump of earth. Consider this man who raised himself to the pinnacle of human values. We too shall come to this. You and I. One day we shall die." Such is the way of all flesh. Here on earth, all is vanity.

T HE BODY is no longer seen. It has disappeared under the earth to rot there in peace, carefully boxed. However, though invisible it still manifests its power once again, and sumptuously so. In the most earthly manner—nourishing, presenting food and drink, giving others occasion to rejoice. According to custom, it presides over a final banquet, as the master of the house, the seigneur who is never better loved than when he distributes bread and wine. He has told his heir that he desires that one hundred poor men be present, and be fed. Let them eat and drink with him. Or rather, from him. For such indeed is the function of these posthumous *agapes*: the dead man's soul requires that the living pray for it, and the food distributed after the burial can be regarded as the payment for these prayers, perhaps even more profoundly, as their equivalent. Of poor men there are on this day many more than are needed. For three months they have impatiently awaited the end of the death agony. Here they all are, hands out. No one dreams of counting them. The mob is so dense that it cannot keep within London's gates, near the sepulcher. The ceremony must be shifted to the open spaces of Westminster in order to proceed with the distribution of moneys and provender, upon which the dramaturgy of the funeral concludes.

The funeral was magnificent, in accordance with the honor of the earl of Pembroke. Not everyone died so well. So William himself might have concluded some thirty years before almost to the day, when the king his lord perished, grandfather of the present king, another Henry, Henry II of England, Henry Plantagenet the Proud, a new King Arthur who had once carried off Eleanor of Aquitaine from the Capetian and who in his time was mighty among the mighty. The earl had not forgotten him. Many a time, he told among his people what he preserved in his memory. With his own eyes, he had seen the sovereign gradually devoured by that disease which had taken him by the heel, risen along his thighs, invaded his whole body, burning him everywhere. He had seen the king drag himself about like an animal, moaning with pain, and knowing that Richard, his eldest son, his heir, his enemy, furious to see him so long in dying, went sneering among the courtiers of the king of France; "The old man is acting out his farce." He had seen him turn red, then black. He was not present when death cracked the king's heart, when the clotted blood ran from his nose to his mouth, but he was told that the dying man lay quite alone. All his friends had fled, tugging here, tugging there, taking with them what they could, abandoning the body to the household riffraff. And he told, too, before dying himself, that the "snatchers" had snatched indeed: Henry had nothing left but his underclothes and his breeches. A few men of great loyalty, and William was among them, hurried to him then, ashamed of what they saw, and flung their cloaks over the corpse. Which was buried then, and properly of course. But the next day the legions of poor men were waiting at the bridge of Chinon, sure of one thing: they would eat. And there was nothing in the king's house, not even a crust of bread. The earl asked whether there were any moneys: no trace of such a thing. And on the bridge, they could hear the poor men's anger swelling, shouting against the scandal, and threatening to destroy everything. The poor had reason to protest. Shame to the dead king who did not feed his people.

On May 14, 1219, William Marshal fed the poor better than a king. It was a king who would speak his eulogy, a fact that gave his relatives no little pride. That king, precisely, who had humbled the pride of the Plantagenets, who had defeated the emperor in battle, as well, at Bouvines five years before, and whose power henceforth spread over the world, dominating with such assurance that he was nicknamed, like the Roman emperors of ancient times, Augustus: Philip, second of that name, king of France. This sovereign was holding court in Gâtinais when the news reached him of the death of William Marshal, whom he had always held in great affection. In company with his relatives and his noble barons, he completed his dinner. The less exalted lords who had served him at table were beginning their own meal. Among them sat Richard, William's second son; he would suffer great grief. The king took care to wait until he had finished eating. Then, before the watchful assemblage, the king turned toward Guillaume des Barres, his friend: "Have you heard what this messenger has told me?" "What is that, sire?" "By my faith, he has come to tell me that the earl, that loyal man, is dead and buried." "Which earl is that, sire?" "The earl of Pembroke, William, who was valiant and wise." "In our time, there was no better knight anywhere, and none who was more diligent in arms." "What is it you say?" "I say, and I call upon God as my witness, that I have never seen a better knight than he in all my life." Guillaume des Barres knew what he was about: he was the most valiant at the court of France, which is to say, in the world. In his day he had rivaled the earl in bravery and in valor; before the walls of Saint-Jean-d'Acre, he had even jousted against Richard Coeur de Lion. It fell to him to accord the deceased a first title, that of military and sportive mastery. King Philip, who officially presided over the council and knew the value of manly friendship, that cement of the feudal state, crowned loyalty thus: "William Marshal was, in my judgment, the most loyal man and true I have ever known, in any country I have been." Lastly, Jean de Rouvray, one of those who stood closest to the king at Bouvines, who protected the royal body with Guillaume des Barres and the comrades of their

25

youth, celebrated the earl's wisdom: "Sire, I judge that this was the wisest knight that was ever seen, in any land, in our age." Skied upon valor, praised on one hand for loyalty, on the other for wisdom, here is knighthood, the highest order created by God. In these courts of valor gathered around the Capetian king, God's first lieutenant upon earth, William Marshal, the most valiant, the most loyal, and the wisest, is thus proclaimed the greatest knight, the flower of chivalry.

2

DURING THE sacred performance whose faithful execu-
tant he had proved to be, thereby carrying out his father's wishes, young William had assumed the leading role
after that of the deceased. Once the earl had taken to his bed,
the son had virtually never left his side, had almost never
slept. Henceforth he was to fill the empty place, and on his
shoulders rested that lineal glory that old William had so
swiftly, by his own virtues, raised to an almost royal status.
It was incumbent on his successor to increase such honor in
his turn, or at least not to permit its luster to be tarnished.
His first duty, then, was to fix the founder's image so deeply
in men's minds that it could resist the wear of time, never
entirely fading, and from age to age show his posterity how
a man should conduct himself. This image, of course, had
been preserved in a number of those communities of priests
or monks, one of whose functions—assuredly the main one
to a layman's eyes—consisted in praying for the dead till the
end of time. Perhaps, too, it was preserved by the ornaments
of the sepulcher. William Marshal's tomb in the Temple in
London vanished before it could be described by antiquari-
ans; there is every reason to believe it was covered with ex-
pressive signs, with commemorative figures. It was the
custom of that age to place such things upon the tombs of
the rich. Yet still more was needed—people could not remain
in a place of prayer forever. Another memorial had to be
built, a secular one capable of circulating the dead man's
renown within the social space in which he had been illus-

trious and from which he had never departed except—a few days before giving up the ghost—when he had assumed the habit of the Templars; it was appropriate to exhibit his glory in princely courts and in the encampments erected beside tournament grounds. Hence it was important that William Marshal's valor be celebrated in the specific forms of a culture that had been his own, that of all his friends, and one he had labored to exalt: the culture of chivalry. Such forms, at the time, were generally so volatile that nothing of them has survived to our own time but the text of a few songs. The monument young William decided to erect to his father's memory was, precisely, a song.

The intention was to keep the deceased present—by words. But not, as in the case of images associated with the funerary cult, by exhibiting a static portrait, by describing with great precision the singular features of his face and figure, by representing the hero's physical person. The song very summarily evokes the earl's appearance, the *faiture* of his body. It tells nothing about him that is not quite common-place: delicate feet, fine hands; well-made, upright in his person; strong of stature. Save that he was brown in both hair and complexion—which was not praise: saints and heroes were recognized by their blondness, by the pallor of their skin; in this age, the notion of sin, of poverty was stubbornly attached to blackness, to darkness—and that his *enfourchure*, his crotch, was very large. But at the beginning of the thirteenth century, the plastic arts, increasingly devoted to a legible figuration, were not yet concerned with likeness; they showed, chiefly, actions. The poem composed to the earl's glory also describes actions—his "gestes." *Chanson de geste:* the expression is appropriate, since this poem was written if not in the form—here it takes that of the *romans*—at least in the spirit of those copious epics, a long series of verses, for example, recounting the various exploits of another William, William of Orange, the short-nosed. The earl lives again in the detailed and precise relation of the vicissitudes of his existence. This biography was produced to be listened to—it was recited publicly by a professional reader. In what circumstances? In what manner? We have no clue. All we know is that it was offered to the attention of his nearest relatives. The donor took care to have inscribed, in the final section, the fact that he had had the work created for his brothers and sisters, seeking to "delight" them by letting them "hear . . . the great merits and the honor of their ancestor," adding that he owed them this gift as their elder and as the heir, and that he doubted not of their gratitude.

Was it exceptional in well-endowed lineages thus to exalt the posthumous image of the head of the household? We do not know, as we do not know how long, around 1220, the custom prevailed of placing an image of the deceased lords upon their tombs. For half a century in the cathedral of Le Mans, there had been, fixed in the enamel, not the portrait but the effigy of Geoffrey Plantagenet. Moreover, there was closely associated with this image a biography, which has also been preserved. But Geoffrey Plantagenet was the father, grandfather, and great-grandfather of the five kings of England whom William Marshal had successively served. Was it not to this eminent quality that he owed his survival in this form? Did not such representations remain a monopoly that the sovereigns of the time, because they had been anointed and crowned, shared with bishops and saints? And if a scribe was commissioned to relate the "gestes" of William Marshal, was it not because the earl had so closely approached the royal power; because, as regent, he had for a while taken the monarch's very place? The song would testify, then, to the pride attached to an extraordinary success, if not to the impudence of a parvenu. Yet why not suppose that among the very high nobility to which his valor had raised him, the earl was no exception; that in accordance with the ritual of aristocratic mourning during this period, many other lives besides his had been sung, but that all trace of these poetic evocations has been lost, because such productions were rarely committed to writing and because, in the residences of the great families, writing was not carefully preserved? Especially since this particular writing, of profane and private intention, was not in Latin?

The memory preserved of the kings of this period, of Philip Augustus as of Geoffrey Plantagenet, was encased in this hieratic language, the Latin of ecclesiastical liturgies and "authors" of erudite literature. Latin imposed respect; it was appropriate for royal eulogies: anointed kings were half churchmen, and Suetonius had composed the model eulogy, the *Lives of the Twelve Caesars*, in Latin. But the accounts of the deeds of barons, meant to be heard by men and women who were anything but scholars, were doubtless more apt to employ a language these people might understand, the one they used, if not every day, at least in the courts where knighthood gathered and where manners that distinguish the wellborn from commoners were indispensable. The author of the Earl's *chanson* uses, in any case, the speech of the good society of England and of its kings, who were Angevin. This is the dialect of western France. Hence this poem, which was composed on the banks of the Thames, is one of the first monuments of French literature. And it is the earliest biography that has been preserved in that language. Extremely vulnerable, the work might well have been lost—like so many others.

As a matter of fact, the earl's line rapidly died out. This was frequently the case in the ruling class, as a consequence of excessively prudent measures which, in order to limit the division of fortunes and to maintain the coherence of estates, forbade most of the sons to marry, thereby reducing the number of legitimate births but also dangerously curbing the expansion of the line. Yet William's posterity seemed to be secure: of the children he had begotten upon his wife, ten survived him, five of whom were sons. One after the other, the sons died without progeniture. Young William perished only twelve years after his father, in 1231; Richard, three years later; Gilbert, who was a cleric, then left the ecclesiastical state, buckled on the sword, assumed the titles, and died of a fall from his horse in 1241 without having begotten a legitimate heir. There then remained only Anselm, the youngest—whom the earl, as he lay dying, had abandoned to his fate, judging that he had no chance whatever of inheriting; upon him fell the succession. His fortune was brief: by 1245 he was dead. No man was left to bear the name of Marshal. Who then would henceforth trouble to preserve his memory? Now, by the greatest stroke of luck, the text of this story survives. In a single manuscript, it is true, and one that is not the original, though the poor transcription (the copyist doubtless had difficulty with a language too refined for his training) seems contemporary with it. Perhaps the copy was commissioned by one of the sisters, or by a nephew, on the occasion, for example, of a marriage. Or perhaps someone interested in history wanted to preserve a narrative that seemed so instructive about the events of his own times and that he considered deserving, for its stylistic qualities, of a place in a well-stocked library. The poem may also have owed its survival to its rare beauty. Masterpieces have a tenacious life.

ONE HUNDRED twenty-seven parchment leaves—not one is missing; on each, two columns of thirty-eight lines; nineteen thousand nine hundred and fourteen verses: young William had done things well. It took seven years to gather the material, to elaborate, to edit the work. The business was a costly one. He who paid for it made sure there was no mistake as to who had done so; it would be clearly expressed. The eldest son, "who sustained thereof the whole cost," was thus the originator. Not the author—this he could not be, for lack of leisure and specifically of competence. Hence he engaged an artisan whose trade was to compose such songs, one of those men who make their living by finding, *de trouver: a trouvère*. Of this man "who made and found this book" we know a name, Jean, but not the surname that would permit us to identify him.

He is a splendid writer: words both accurate and fresh, narration limpid, characterizations vivid, dialogues pointed, scenes clear; he has performed his task to perfection: to render the earl "present," to make him "alive." Moreover, he reveals himself to be a very conscientious historian. The work is presented as a "life," but also as an *estoire*, a history. Its author shares the concern lately manifested in monasteries and collegiate churches by those committed to relating the stories they were told, to verify their information, to criticize the testimony with the same conscientiousness shown by historians today. Jean is careful to indicate his sources. Several times over, we find him setting forth his scruples and the standards of veracity he imposes on himself. Thus when he recounts the progress at the battle of Lincoln, which saw the earl victorious as a king, the event is a crucial one; the hero's career and the entire action that the poem has followed step by step culminate on this day. It is important to see clearly, to say nothing that is not absolutely certain. At this point, Jean the Anonymous inserts his profession of faith: "Here, lords, what must I say? Those who inform me are not in agreement among themselves; I cannot obey each and all; I should lose my way; the true path would be hidden from me, and I should be the less believed. In history, which is truth, no one may knowingly tell a lie." His employers were expecting a sincere report. The writer has therefore striven to distinguish true from false among the traces the earl's actions had left.

But it was also important that the report be copious, detailed, fleshed out. Hence the writer has conscientiously gone about collecting all these traces, scraping up even their minutest vestiges. His concern that this harvest be complete explains why he has taken so many years to execute the commission. However, as a *trouvère*, he did not stuff himself full of what was in the texts of learned libraries. This independence is evident when we compare his accounts with those of the chroniclers to whom he could readily have referred, and who, moreover, pillage each other so consistently; there is not the slightest coincidence between their versions and his own that might allow us to presume that he read them. He drew upon other sources that, without him, would have remained inaccessible to us, for they are located on the secular side of thirteenth-century culture. Of this aspect of cultural creation, almost everything has evaporated. It escapes us. Which is why the *chanson* so enthralls me. The work of a man who did not belong to the clerical intelligentsia, or who at least turned away from it during the course of his work, it bears exceptional witness to what was, among the knights of the period, the meaning and the knowledge of history. It is the determination of a memory that I shall not even call courtly, for in the great princely courts the weight of ecclesiastical influences on secular ways of thinking was notably greater than in William's household. What is given us is infinitely precious: the memory of chivalry in an almost pure state, about which, without this evidence, we should know virtually nothing.

According to him, it is his own memory that Jean le Trouvère has searched. While writing the biography, he was probably established in the household of young William. But if we do not take as a stylistic device or a simple slip of the pen the fact that he sometimes intervenes personally at the end of a line, declaring "this I have seen" or "I remember that," we can suppose that this writer might well be one of those heralds-of-arms who arranged the jousts on the tournament grounds, identified the protagonists by their insignia, and by singing their exploits boosted the reputation of the champions. And that, like other specialists of knightly advertising, he was occasionally to be found among the intimates of the earl, who paid well. Further, since the matters

33

that the author claims, by such notations, to have witnessed directly date back to around 1180, the poem must have been written by a man already well on in years. The particular Norman dialect he employs confirms the fact; it is so filled with archaisms that it might easily pass for a work composed thirty years earlier, at the end of the twelfth century. It is also confirmed by Jean's insistence—but is this not a contemporary commonplace of courtly literature?—to mourn times past when everything, he says, was finer.

Nonetheless, in all essentials, what he calls the *matière*, the raw material he is working up, comes to him from others. When in the last lines he supplies credits for the work and implores God to give "the joy of paradise" to those who have leagued together for its completion, he refers to three persons: the patron—that is, William, "the good son"; the maker—that is, himself; and finally a third man who, out of love, the *bon amour* of his lord, furnishes information, dedicating to this task "his heart, his thought and his holdings" —Jean. Along with Paul Meyer, editor of this text, I believe that this is not the same Jean. This one is clearly identified; we have met him just now, closer than anyone else to the dying earl—John d'Erley. The surname he bears designates a Berkshire village near Reading, and near Caversham as well. John therefore came from the countryside where the earl was born. He possessed lands there. Perhaps he was a distant relative. He makes his appearance in the narrative in 1188, during the capture of Montmirail, in Maine. At the time he was the earl's squire, his assistant. He took care of the armor, the charger, carried the shield. Such functions normally fell to young men, apprentices of the military profession; William had been in the same position twenty years earlier. At this time, John d'Erley had just entered his service. The earl had taken him on when he returned from the Holy Land; previously, he had had Eustace de Bertrimont as his squire. Like William long ago, like Eustace lately, John soon became a knight, but did not leave his master. He followed him step by step, sharing the same fortunes. Thus he too gradually raised himself to his present rank; King John, in particular, heaped him with favors. Yet it seems that he remained "young," in the sense this word had in the knights' language: he never married. In any case he died childless; in 1231 his brother Henry succeeded to his entire estate. All his life John was bound to William Marshal by what the poem calls love.

A very strong word: manly friendship at its peak. It justifies the role that John d'Erley here takes. He is the informant *par excellence*. The poem's substance is essentially constituted by what has filled his memory during the thirty-one years he served the deceased. It would seem that the poet, when he sets himself to versifying this accumulation, utilizes it in some written form. Does he not indicate as much several times over: "the writing says what I here say," "this is what the writing tells me"? If he did not read the church chroniclers, he nonetheless worked—this is certain—on parchments, such as that ancient account that was preserved in the household archives and that he made use of in order to specify what the earl had won during a tournament. But also this other text, or rather these other texts of which he speaks, and which diverge, he tells us, apropos of the battle of Lincoln; the substance of the *Histoire*, then, was not entirely an orally transmitted memory. In any case, if we abide by what the author asserts, at least a part of the memory he was commissioned to elaborate had previously been transferred from oral to written form—already fixed in notes. Could it be that John d'Erley had himself begun to celebrate the glory of his lord and benefactor at his own expense (since it is clearly stated that he put his "holdings" into the enterprise), dictating to scribes what he remembered? Perhaps. At least there is no doubt that the surest material comes from John d'Erley, the earl's alter ego, who survives him and who speaks. Telling what he has seen with his own eyes but also, and perhaps especially, what the earl, when he was alive, used to tell and like to hear told. John d'Erley's memory is in reality that of William Marshal himself. John was the accredited bearer of this memory; he bears it still after the earl's death and polishes it, as once he had borne and polished the arms of his lord and master. He hands it over, glistening, when he is asked to do so. As a faithful servant, loving his master. Out of John's mouth—his junior by some twenty years—William himself speaks. The substance comes from him, from his own memory. Ultimately, what is the *chanson* but his memoirs, not personally written, but spoken and faithfully reported? An autobiography? The equivalent of those confessions that intellectuals like Guibert de Nogent and Abelard had undertaken to write a century earlier, modeled on Saint Augustine's *Confessions?* Is not what we have here the personal memoirs of a knight contemporary with Eleanor of Aquitaine and of Philip Augustus? Let us take advantage of this windfall.

ᛏHESE MEMOIRS are astonishingly faithful. As were, a hundred years later, with an incredible precision as to the details of the thing seen, those of Joinville, who, when even older than John d'Erley, ransacked his past with the same intention: to resuscitate his deceased master, repeating the words Saint Louis had uttered, recalling his attitudes, the color of his garments, he too dictating to a scribe. An exact, infallible, prodigiously rich memory, the memory of all the men of this period who did not read, did not write. (William Marshal, as we know, was illiterate. One day his friend Baldwin de Béthune gave him a letter to carry; William had it read to him by a cleric, who performed his task very well, "word by word," the song says, "without skipping a thing.") Consequently, these men had to rely entirely on what their minds filed away, and hence were careful not to let this natural faculty atrophy, unconsciously training it by constant exercise, by the practice of singing (William enjoyed singing), by recitation, by miming, by brooding over the words they heard.

Of this faithful memory, the relation is sincere. We can verify it. Paul Meyer, who produced an admirable edition of the *Histoire* in three volumes, published for the Société de l'Histoire de France in 1891, 1894, and 1901, accompanied the text with a copious, precise commentary that enables us to check almost every detail. Some thirty years later, Sidney Painter, one of the best American medievalists and one of the first seriously to study the culture of chivalry, explored the archives even more minutely; his book, *William Marshal, Knight-errant, Baron and Regent of England*, published in Baltimore in 1933, furnishes all the complementary materials to be desired. I rely upon these two monuments of erudition and feel quite comfortable in doing so, for they convince me that nothing the *chanson* relates is contradicted by what was written in the period and has come down to us, chronicles or titles, deeds, and charters. What distortions there are derive primarily from the fact that this literary document is a panegyric, as were the lives of saints and kings, a defense *pro domo*, as memoirs always are. It exaggerates the subject's virtues, of course, focusing all the attention on them and carefully keeping the less glorious side of things in obscurity, erasing whatever might dim the image's luster. This was one of the functions of this family literature—to defend the interests of the house by exonerating those members whose conduct was under attack, making heroes of the cowardly, the cunning, and the perverse by exalting their supposed virtues and contradicting all rumors that tended to vilify them. On occasion, apology went too far. And that may be the case here. If it seemed necessary, after 1219, to parade William's loyalty (*loyal*, of course, rhymes with *Maréchal*), was this not because it was crucial to smother any rumors of treachery? In any case, we possess the evidence: his reputation did not have the excellence the poem's author attributes to it, and many in England were to speak of betrayal of a suzerain's duty, of perfidy. Let us take the eulogy for what it is without being deceived by it.

The other defect results from lapses of memory. Forgetting undermines its initial foundations. Once attention ventures outside the period when John d'Erley could be a direct witness, we see the collapse of that rigor that for more immediate epochs maintains in exact linear continuity the vector on which deeds and events are situated in their proper place. And memory frays, losing all coherence, when Jean le Trouvère no longer dares say "I have seen," when the events he relates are more than forty years old. Before 1188, the vision grows blurred; it fades altogether earlier than 1180. Such a reproach, in truth, is a minor one with regard to the goal I am pursuing. Indeed, I am less concerned with facts than with the way in which facts were remembered and spoken of. I am not writing the history of events. That history is written, and extremely well. My concern is to shed light on what is still very dimly seen, drawing on this testimony, whose exceptional value I have indicated, for what it teaches us of the culture of chivalry. I want to try to see the world the way these men saw it.

It is men I speak of: this is a masculine world, and in it only males count. This primary, this fundamental feature must be emphasized from the start; very few feminine figures occur in this poem, and their appearances are fugitive. The only women who take the stage even briefly are those related —and very closely—to the hero: mother, sisters, wife, daughters: the core family, the circle governed by the incest taboo, not according to the Church's rules, which extended this ban much further, but according to the popular morality observed during the period. Even these very close relatives remain shadows, barely glimpsed. Of William's mother, we are told no more than her name and the illustrious house from which she comes, and that she had her heart set on sending one of her own people for news of her little boy who had been taken prisoner. We have already observed the place taken by the wife: marginal. She appears, with her daughters, only during the long deathbed sequence. Occasionally summoned by the men, these women enter the room where the earl lies dying; they do not remain there long, they do not speak there; nothing of what they might have said, in any case, seemed worthy of being reported; all the dialogues are among men. The women weep, they swoon, they play the part suited to their sex in such circumstances. There remains that touch of feeling, on the part of the dying man, for his companion of twenty years, and for the least provided-for of his daughters. In his turn he weeps for them. And these are the only tears we see him shed. But nowhere is it shown that he has been concerned with these women before the scene of farewells. Unless apropos of the betrothals—his and those of the four older daughters. Apropos of marriages, which is to say, of serious matters. And these matters are dealt with by men, among themselves.

On occasion we glimpse, passing through the narrative, other women. I have counted, all in all, seven such appearances, most of them extremely brief, generated by the development of the narrative itself. In describing the hero's death, room had to be made for the daughters who respectfully visit their dying father and respectfully wait for his last breath. In the same way, it is fitting, in the vicissitudes of that specifically masculine sport constituted by military prowess, that a few feminine characters intervene now and then. A few who are directly involved, since it happens that women take part in such occasions. But are these in fact really women? Stripped of all femininity, they actually join combat in the fashion of men. Like that Dame Nicole who had inherited Lincoln castle: she defended it with all her might against the men of Prince Louis of France. Or like the less wellborn but equally fervent bourgeoises of Drincourt (today Neufchâtel-en-Bray). In this town, the French and Norman knights were at grips, when the latter gained the upper hand; at which point the women followed their men out of the houses and pursued the French in disarray, armed with clubs, staves, axes. Previously, these amazons, accompanied by the ladies of the nobility, had clustered at the windows and on the balconies. From the beginning of the engagement, they had followed the phases of the battle as impassioned spectators.

It must be said the poem describes this battle in the fashion usually employed for tournaments, with heralds, minstrels counting the blows, and an attentive audience of supporters. As a matter of fact, in the uncertainty I have mentioned, since this event is kept in the background of memory, the hero is supposed to have been armed as a knight on that day. This is why the skirmish is treated as one of those festivals during which the newly dubbed knights give evidence of their valor, parading before their admiring women. In truth, the story of William Marshal suggests that women, in those days, did not attend the tournaments so often as is presumed. The narrative I am using is filled to overflowing with descriptions of tournaments, yet the presence of women is mentioned—and on the margins of the action—in only two of these combats. At Pleurs, in Champagne, it is noted after the combat's conclusion: a woman of noble birth, with kindly intentions, comes to offer the duke of Burgundy, sponsor of one of the teams, a wondrous fish, a pike over six feet long. This symbolic object constituted the prize, awarded to the victor. (It is notable, of course, that it is incumbent upon a woman to award it, and this feature is likely to comfort those who believe in the promotion of woman in the twelfth century, complacently imagining, in a troubadoresque setting, picturesque beauties crowning their champions.) When one is a prince and noble of heart, one does not keep such gifts for oneself, one distributes them to others whom one insists one regards as more valiant than oneself. As did the duke of Burgundy, "in order to multiply twice over the honor" of the lady, who was courteous, learned and, the poem tells us, valiant herself, the fine object therefore passed from hand to hand among the upper barony, to end up, of course, in the earl's own.

At the even more brilliant tournament of Joigny, the ladies appear at the outset. The team of which the earl is captain is already prepared and awaits the starting signal in the lists. Whereupon out of the castle comes the countess, "well-made in face and person, escorted by ladies and maidens, all elegant, courteous, and in fine array." The knights no longer contain themselves, and break ranks; they dash forward to the encounter in fine fettle, drawn by this lure, spurred on by the vision of these delightful creatures, "the hardihood redoubles in their hearts." A feminine power—this time, incontestable. Yet let us consider more closely what role is assigned to women. They are present in order to excite the warriors to greater valor. Under their gaze, the fighting will be all the more ardent; the war, or the simulacrum of war, then assumes the guise of a competition of males, of one of those biological mechanisms. At Joigny, however, the women have a different function: to distract the men, to help them pass the time when this time hangs heavy, and when, not being in the lists to fight, the knight in his armor does not know what to do with himself. As a matter of fact, it comes straightaway—as always, it is the men alone who speak—"Let us go to it, let us dance, to beguile the tedium of the waiting." The scene is worth noting carefully, for we do not often have an occasion to observe how people danced in those days. Men and women take each other by the hand for something like a round dance. There are no musicians; only singing sustains the steps. "Who will have the courtesy to sing?" The earl, of course. He intones a song for leading voice, and all accompany him. Courtesy: it was to be expected in a work rhymed in the fashion of the *romans* of the very period when Guillaume de Lorris was composing the *Roman de la Rose*, taking pains to describe the pleasures that a man of good birth enjoys in this life. Yet I should note how

41

discreet is the presence of this courtesy: throughout such prolonged, such indulgent descriptions of the military encounters, only a single allusion is made to the interludes when, for diversion, the knights concern themselves a moment with women of their rank. And even here, attention is not focused on the latter. Are we sure, in fact, that William, exhibiting his talents as a singer, was trying to please the countess and her ladies rather than asserting by another kind of prowess his pre-eminence over his fighting comrades, extending among the ladies a contest of virile excellence that generally played itself out among men only?

Whatever the case, during some twenty thousand lines we are shown but three women who, without being his close relatives, had a direct connection with the earl. Here they are. The first to appear in a narrative is a lady, a noble's wife who takes pity on William when, still very young and seriously wounded, he is being dragged by his Augustinian captors from one hiding place to the next, in order to keep his own people from recovering him. At one of these furtive halts, a woman of quality, "liberal and debonair," gazes upon him one evening at a distance. Love? Desire, perhaps? Was this woman one of those unsatisfied wives whom God, to test His future saints, induced, according to the hagiographers, to pursue the youths taking a night's shelter in their castles? Whatever the case, it is esteem that the *trouvère* advances here as the sole motive. The lady questions; she is told what proofs of courage the youth has just manifested: he has put his body in danger in order to avenge his murdered uncle. She sends someone to inquire after his needs: some cloth, to dress the wound; she sends him shredded linen by stealth inside a loaf of bread she has hollowed out, cunning as overly tender-hearted women are known to be. But without our being told whether or not she herself has approached the youth: no woman's hands tended William, but his own, transformed for this purpose into those of a surgeon.

The second story is one of love, though our hero is neither its subject nor its object. He is riding, accompanied only by Eustace, his squire, toward Montmirail where two of his knightly companions await him, Baldwin de Béthune and Hugh de Hamelincourt. On the way he is overcome by a need for sleep; he stretches out beside the way, perhaps on the edge of the Roman road, ordering the horses to be unbridled so that they can graze freely. He dozes off. A noise awakens him: a woman's voice, very close to him, saying— and this is the only woman in the entire poem whose words we hear—"Ah, God, how weary I am." She is not alone. Opening his eyes, William catches sight of a couple passing, riding two fat palfreys "of good cognizance" and loaded with bulging saddlebags. The man is of fine appearance and confident gestures, the lady fair and certainly of quality. Both are wearing capes of fine Flemish cloth—very elegant. "Eustace, what is it I hear? Bridle my horse, I would know whence these come and where they are going." (It is only polite, as a matter of fact, to speak to those one passes on the road, when they are people of quality.) In his haste, William forgets his sword. Joining the knight, he grasps him by the sleeve of his mantle, questions him. "Who might you be?" "A man." "I see for myself that you are no beast." The other pulls himself away and prepares to unsheathe: "If you are looking for a fight, you shall have one." (The dialogue, which I am following virtually word for word, is by Jean le Trouvère.) "Eustace, my sword!" The stranger drops his mantle, puts up his sword, and takes himself off. He is immediately caught, he struggles, his hood falls off and he is discovered to be tonsured: a monk, and the handsomest that can be imagined. Filled with shame and dread, he surrenders: "We are at your mercy. I am a monk, as you can see. And the lady is *mon amie* [We must note the word: not his wife or his bride.] I have carried her off from her own country. We are journeying into foreign parts." In tears, the girl confesses that she is Flemish, a sister of Monseigneur Raoul de Lens. "You cannot be in

43

your wits to wander thus," William protests. (It is inconceivable that a girl of good family should take to the roads like a harlot; the only tolerable wanderers are knights.) "Give over such madness. I shall return you to your brother: he is an acquaintance of mine." But she: "Never shall I be seen again in a country where I am known." William does not insist, but is disturbed; are they well supplied? Have they moneys of any kind? The monk shows a belt bulging with coins; here, he boasts, he has at least forty-eight pounds; this money shall be put out at interest. In a thriving city they will live upon the income. "Upon usury? By God's sword, you shall not. Eustace, take possession of the money." This done, the couple is free to depart. "Since they refuse to mend their ways, since their wrongfulness beguiles them still," William sends them to the devil. Eustace is ordered to say nothing of all this when William rejoins his friends. They were beginning to lose patience, hungry as they were. In order to raise their spirits, William tosses the money-belt upon the inn table. The coins are counted, nor had the monk lied: over ten thousand *deniers*, enough to buy very fine things indeed. After eating and drinking, William tells where the windfall came from. Hugh protests; the miscreants had not been stripped of their steeds and their baggage. "As for that, bring me my horse, I shall follow and broach the matter to them." William dissuades him, determined that affairs should remain where they are.

The anecdote is of the kind people enjoyed repeating to the aging earl. Its lesson is of great interest for the historian of manners. It shows him what almost all the sources he can consult have concealed, except for the fictive ones, which he rightly considers with a critical eye: the daughters of noble houses were not all obedient; it sometimes happened that their loves were far-ranging, that certain couples formed without parental consent. Orphaned daughters, objects of exchange between their brothers and their likely bridegrooms, were sometimes determined to marry themselves off on their own. There were known occasions, perhaps less exceptional than we tend to suppose, of rape, of elopement, of clandestine engagements. In short, it was seen that love might contradict the schemes of the heads of families. It was not impossible after the fact, by the intervention of friends, to arrange matters, to pacify resentments, to reconcile the *demoiselles* with those whose control they had escaped, to restore them, a little the worse for wear, to the regular circuit of matrimonial exchanges. On condition, of course, that they themselves agreed to such conduct. By this story we note that some such girls, whether out of shame or ruled by their passions, did not let themselves be restored to decorum, that there were stubborn daughters who sought to run their own lives at whatever cost.

The knight's ethic—this, on the other hand, is very familiar to us—obliged him to ride at full tilt to the rescue of wellborn women when he found them in danger. Indeed, as soon as the sound of feminine distress, which he interprets as a call for help, comes to his ears, William leaps up. But the knight's ethic also forbade him to force his will upon women. In matters of love, he must respect their will. Moreover, the Church enjoins him to do as much. Is not the conjugal link, blessed by the Lord, bound fast by the heart's adherence and by mutual consent? William, a perfect knight, consequently masters himself and his impulses: he leaves the *amie* to her friend. Yet he is not content; this friend is a monk. A mockery. He is not accustomed to pay much attention to monks at this flourishing time in his life. Yet that a girl of good family should offer a monk her body disgusts him. A cleric, at the limit, and even then . . . Chivalry undertakes to keep all women of noble blood for itself; it jealously forbids them to males of other condition. As did the troubador Count William of Poitiers, William judges that ladies and maidens who do not reject all other love but the love of knights deserve the stake, or some other fire. Of course, in accordance with the precept of the peace of God, he does not believe he possesses the right to lay hands upon the guilty woman. Nor upon her lover: a knight's mission is not to enforce monastic vows. At least he takes whatever opportunity to chastise comes his way: the money, all they have. Yet it burns his hands, he will not touch it, ordering his squire to take it for him. This booty will serve for knightly pleasures, and the knight spends it with a free heart—indeed, he would be ashamed to stint. It matters little how such money was acquired. The loathsome thing is that this tonsured fellow, who takes a noble girl to his bed, should claim to use it, even as a bourgeois might do, by putting it out at interest. A man of quality does not "profit" in this fashion. He profits by his valor, by seizing his prey at the risk of his body, not by exploiting others' needs by lending—in particular, as he knows, to knights, to improvident knights at usurious rates. William therefore loots the monk with a clear conscience. Taking only the coins, "saving" them from a wrong purpose by putting them to the only use that is not malodorous: for festive expenditures. Taking anything more would be . . . brigandage. But this particular distraint seems honorable to him, as to those who for his glory propagated the memory of his good actions. As for the woman, he has not touched her either. He has treated this wicked creature according to the laws of chivalry.

Lastly—and here is the third and final figure of a woman who occurs in the narrative, but an impalpable one, scarcely to be seen. She is not named; we do not glimpse her face; she is present only in the discourse of the men in the dispute of which she is the object: this time, a love attributed to William, a culpable love. In 1182—he is at least thirty-five—he is not yet married; he is, as was said at the time, a *bachelier*, but already famous, hence envied by his closest companions, the men of war who, like him, belong to the great military household constituted for young Henry, heir to the English throne, whom his father, Henry Plantagenet, has caused to be anointed and crowned, associating him with his power. There are five men who envy William. Three of them the poet does not name; when he writes, their line is not yet extinguished. He names only Adam d'Iqueboeuf and Thomas de Coulonces. The five seek to destroy their comrade because their lord loves him too much. This is indeed what they envy him for: the great love of which he is the object. Thus, this entire episode turns on love, but let there be no mistake: it is the love of men among themselves. This no longer surprises us; we are beginning to discover that love *à la courtoise*, the love celebrated, after the troubadors, by the *trouvères*, the love that the knights devoted to the chosen lady, may have masked the essential—or rather, projected into the realm of sport the inverted image of the essential: amorous exchanges between warriors.

The story is a long one. I am examining it in all the details the poem affords. Not only because the earl told it or liked to hear it, but particularly for the harsh light it casts on the reality of the relations between masculine and feminine at the end of the twelfth century, in the great courts whose princes offered to entertain their invited friends by reading them the *romans bretons*. The envious five (the *losengiers*, as Jean the Anonymous calls them, using the storytellers' term) therefore concoct a plot that will spread among the master's favorites who dispute his favors and spy on each other's advancement. It will end by transforming the love of the lord into a "great and cruel hatred" toward the man they seek to destroy. Yet, taking care not to be hated themselves, they shall merely sow suspicion. Adam and Thomas are Normans. They begin with another Norman, Raoul de Hamars, counting first of all on his ethnic pride, here touching a very sensitive string: "We are all bastardized, if we continue to let ourselves be done in by this Englishman." No one speaks of anyone else in all Normandy, in all France! And why? Because he has Henry the Norman in his hand—the herald-of-arms who, at the opening of each and every tournament, shouts William's war cry: "*Ça! Dieu aide au Maréchal!*" Thereupon the best rush forward and join his team. He need merely hold out his hand to take horses and knights, all he desires. Whence his chivalry, the renown that eclipses us now, and the money by which he makes so many friends. But this is not what cankers us, even so. We can scarcely believe our ears; it is to the wife of Henry, our lord, that William "does this thing." What thing? Makes love? No, the word does not occur. The word love, throughout the entire *chanson*, never intervenes except between men. What is concerned here is much simpler: William is sleeping with the queen.

The queen, wife of the young King Henry, is Margaret, daughter of King Louis VII of France, the sister of Philip Augustus. In 1168, to consolidate the recently concluded peace between Capetians and Plantagenets, Margaret was given by her father to the son of Henry II. This boy was five years old at the time, and Margaret three. Now she is twenty-five, ten years younger than William. This is all we know about her. And other sources for the poem, as I have said, never even utter her name. She appears in the biography as a kind of abstract sign, a validating attribute, adding to the hero's luster. Adding considerably, it is true. Who, except Tristan perhaps, could dream of a paramour of nobler blood? And even Tristan was the nephew of King Mark. William is far from being able to claim any such relationship. He is merely a knight-errant, like those who are accusing him.

The presumption of adultery is latent in the noble houses. All the young knights (William is not so young as all that, but in the sense of the period he is "young": he is unmarried) lay siege to the lord's wife. This is the sport of courtesy. It adds spice to the permanent competition of which the court is the site. All are rivals. Who will win the lady's love—in order to attract the lord's to himself? But there is a risk of being caught at this sport, of trespassing the lawful bounds. It then becomes dangerous. A woman is anything but protected in these great residences without partitions, dark as soon as night falls, and filled with men. She herself, generally frustrated, has on occasion the hopes of some pleasure of her own. Promiscuity favors conjunctions that are not only for show. Once upon a time, in the house of the king of France, the grandfather and the mother of young Henry, Geoffrey Plantagenet and Queen Eleanor of Aquitaine, may thus have joined their bodies in mortal sin; at least so Geoffrey boasted. In any case, each man believes that such fornications, whether forced or consented to, are possible; the head of the house dreads them, fears seeing attributed to him children born of another stock who will usurp his ancestral possessions; everyone around him is on the watch, eager to keep awake the master's jealousy in order to enjoy his favor, to supplant his comrades. "If the lord king," say Adam and Thomas, "were to know of William Marshal's passion, we should be well revenged upon him." They urge Raoul to reveal the "shame," the "ugliness" by which the king is "disgraced and deceived." A shame that is reflected on his people and by which they regard themselves as degraded.

Prudently, Raoul evades the issue. No more than the *losengiers* is he willing to incur the lord's anger, nor that of the man who is to be betrayed. What does it matter?—the rumor is already running wild; William Marshal has had wind of it from Peter of Préaux. If there is any shame in the matter, he decides, it will be his if he tries to defend himself against the lie. Sure of his innocence, he waits until the truth becomes evident. No one yet dares to speak to the husband. One of the five then thinks of using one of the most serviceable among the men of the household—one of the close relatives, a first cousin on both sides; this is a "page," a little fellow, a boy the king loves (this time, it is a question of love). They make him drink too much, thereby entrapping this Raoul Farci, appropriately named. He babbles to the king, who at first refuses to believe what he has heard. Then the five conspirators emerge from the shadows, bearing the collective testimony that custom requires in order to sustain the accusation against the wife and to open the case. They confirm:

they are so informed "by hearing and by sight." Shaken, which is to say convinced, young Henry acts as he is supposed to act.

With regard to Margaret, the text affords me no word whatever. It is as if she did not exist, as if the men—even her husband—were not at all concerned with her, engaged only by the fluctuations of love and hate among themselves at the heart of the closed masculine world. Was the queen questioned, put to the proof of red-hot iron, customary in such circumstances? We know only that Henry, a few months later, sent her away, like an object he no longer enjoyed using, to her brother, King Philip of France, who was soon to use her again, remarrying her to King Bela of Hungary. But no chronicle tells us that this return had motives other than the hazards of a diplomacy in which marriages and repudiations constituted the most habitual means. As for William, his lord turned his back upon him and spoke to him no longer. He withdrew his love from him. The only punishment, but the worst of all, by which he was cruelly tormented.

Betrayed, or claiming to be, William left the court. Of his own free will, the story tells us. Soon, however, he began to hope once more. Young Henry had need of him: the last tournament of the autumn of 1182 was announced, before the Christmas season put a stop to such games. England's team would have been of little worth if William had not constituted, as on other occasions, its mainstay. Shame and resentment faded before the desire to win once more the guerdon of military prowess. Here we can measure what jealousy could be worth, and women also, by the yardstick of the pleasures the knights expected from life. Thus we see William turning up fully armed at the very moment when, under Plantagenet colors, the knights were about to enter the lists. Without a word William joins them, and among them, all day long, does what was expected of him, performing superbly, even once refraining, in the fashion worthy of a gentleman, from taking possession of horses, riders, caparisons. Twice he goes to the rescue of the man who has not ceased to be his lord, releasing him at the moment he is about to be taken captive. To his deeds, young Henry's side owes its victory. On all sides it is unanimously declared that William is the best knight of the tournament. When, as usual, the noblest barons gather after the meet, the count of Flanders jokingly reproaches the young king: "Fair cousin, when one has a knight like William Marshal, one does not let him stray." Is this a taunt in the count's cups? Has the rumor of adultery spread outside the household? The king makes no reply; he cannot give his reasons and he is seen to blush—and William with him—from shame and anger. Silence separates the two men. Devotion, perfectly rendered services, do not suffice to waken love. Rancor is stronger still, it stifles gratitude. William, therefore, makes his departure alone. Before the lord's wrath, none of his friends dares join company with him.

The envious want more of this. They have seen their lord frown at the victor, but have also discovered that the king cannot do without him. They must therefore strike higher. They proceed to Rouen to inform the young king's father; old Henry trembles beneath the "burden of shame." No more. At heart, quite pleased: the band of wastrels his son supports are leading him astray; if William withdraws from among them, so much the better; that will be one less, and doubtless the most prodigal of the lot. But when William learns that King Henry II of England, whom he knows to be informed of these matters, is to hold plenary court at Caen at Christmas, he hastens to attend. He has now made up his mind to be silent no longer, to exonerate himself publicly and before the noblest audience, the flower of chivalry gathered for the winter festival. This is the place, this the moment to pierce the boil, to settle the quarrel according to rights and, for himself, to do battle like a new Tristan, to undergo ordeal by combat, the judgment of God. God, by the outcome of a judiciary duel, will himself distinguish the innocent from the guilty. Let there even be three successive combats. He says he is ready to confront the three most valorous champions that can be found, one after the next. If he fails to vanquish all three, he is more than willing that the suspicious husband put him to death by hanging. This is what he proposes, in full court, to the man who regards himself as the injured party. Or else to cut off a finger—any finger—of his right hand. He accepts the handicap and will fight in that fashion against any man chosen from among those who accuse him. A new King Mark, young Henry refuses: "I have no part in your quarrel." There is only one character missing from this powerful scene: Iseult. Is she even present? What is astonishing is that such affairs are treated as a great spectacle. There is nothing left for William to do but take his leave. Which he does with great formality. Facing the two kings, old and young: "Since no man raises his head among those who have cast blame upon me, and since thus it is allowed, against the law of the land, since your court is entirely against me, who have nonetheless offered more than my due, I see indeed that I must seek elsewhere the place where I may live a better life. It is my pleasure, at least, that such a gathering can see with its own eyes that my rights have been taken from me." Duly armed with a safe-conduct, he leaves the Plantagenet realm. Sure of himself. A few weeks later, as a matter of fact, the young king sends to beg him to return. Meanwhile, he has rid himself of his wife. Nothing keeps him from loving William, who remains, as it happens, indispensable. He loves him once more. With an indulgence that is astonishing, to our eyes. But was it not incumbent upon kings, incarnating the first of the three functions, that of wisdom, to show, as Georges Dumézil writes in *La Courtisane et les seigneurs colorés*, following the research of Joël Grisward, "a serene tolerance for the weakness of women"?

According to the deceased's panegyric, this rumor was a calumny. William was wrongfully accused, like Susanna by the Elders, deceived like the Magi by Herod, condemned without proof like Daniel in the lions' den. Was he innocent? Secrecy, dissimulation, are *de rigueur* in matters of *courtoisie*. We may assume, in any case, that he was not a little flattered, that he even prided himself on having been, for once in his life, considered the lover of a queen. Had he not incarnated, on the most brilliant of stages and in the finest role, the adventures of the most fascinating of storybook heroes? Who knows if during the rest of his life, the danger past, he defended himself against suspicion as ardently as they would have us believe who later celebrated his virtues? Did he not perhaps enjoy letting a certain doubt hover over him? Without insisting, apparently, on the *amie*, whose chief attraction in his eyes, as in the tale, had been that she was the wife of a king. Was the memory of deeds done, as it is established in the *Histoire de Guillaume le Maréchal*, inflected, and how far, by the echo of the dreams provoked by tales the knights never tired of being told? Certainly I am amazed to see how short the distance is—and this text furnishes our sole occasion for measuring it—between the courtly romances and the reality that the poem claims faithfully to describe. An observation that would suggest that we not regard as so fallacious the image the literature of chivalry affords of the behavior of men and women. In any case, I regard William, in the posture attributed to him by his biography, honored by the quality of the woman whose conquest is attributed to him, as the surest witness of what was, in its social truth, the love that we know as *courtois*. Men's business, a matter of shame and of honor, of virile love (need I constrain myself to speak of mere friendship?). Let me repeat: only men are said to love each other in a narrative from which women are almost entirely absent. A very special literary genre, the funeral apology may have been obliged to observe such discretion. Whatever the case, in what we may regard as his memoirs, William reveals nothing of dealings we ourselves could call amorous. This silence, in and of itself, says a good deal about the state of the feminine condition, or rather about the consideration men had for women in those times.

W OMEN ARE, when men speak of them at all, a negligible quantity. But many men count scarcely more for the earl and his friends. No allusion to those countless hordes whose function was to till the soil. Save one, in passing—apropos of what the peasants were suffering during the wars. Here we must take care: we are being urged, not to take pity on their lot, but to deplore the effects of their poverty: when the poor, pillaged and tyrannized by the soldiers of both sides, no longer have anything to call their own, when they abandon the fields and take to flight, the lords themselves are impoverished. It is they who are to be pitied. No bourgeois occur either, or virtually none, for such men are contemptible: they hoard moneys at the expense of the very knights they exploit. But it is more surprising that the clergy makes virtually no better a showing. We see a few bishops in passing, not the holiest ones, the most learned ones, but the ones who, helmeted, lead the battle with the knights their brothers: the bishop of Dreux, the bishop of Winchester. So long as the earl has any strength left in his body, he apparently chooses to have little to do with clerics or monks. The monument erected to his glory says little of his devotions. No more than of his loves. Which forbids us, let us take note, to assume that he had dealings with women just as seldom. For we know that he was pious in his own way, quite suspicious with regard to specialists in prayer—a piety we may regard as common enough in military circles. William lived surrounded by warriors; they filled his entire memory. Some among them were not nobles: the *ribauds* who fought for money, foot soldiers (as was to be expected of inferiors), loathsome men whose effectiveness was nonetheless acknowledged. Some of these are glimpsed on the outskirts of the scuffles. Nonetheless, the stage is utterly filled with horses and their riders, and all the latter, with the exception of a few "sergeants," are of noble birth. In the eyes of the man whose feats are being described for us, only a portion of the masculine species counts, formed by the combatants worthy of the name, designated by God for this function, and the sword, formally bestowed on the day of their elevation, bears witness to their vocation: the knights.

The earl's eulogy is fundamentally theirs. His praise is amplified for a moment at the narrative's culmination, when the earl describes the moment fortune turned during the Lincoln battles and when heaven granted the victory to William and his companions. We then seem to hear the words that sustained the courage of these men in adversity and bolstered their pride, exalting their courage and their powers in a state they never doubted was the highest of all. Profession of a faith sure of itself and of a scorn no less assured for what lay beneath that state, for any action that was not military.

> What is it, then, to bear arms?
> Does one employ them as one might
> a harrow, a winnowing-fan, an axe?
> No, it is a far more arduous labor.
> What then is chivalry?
> So strong a thing, and of such hardihood,
> and so costly in the learning,
> that a wicked man or low dare not undertake it . . .
> Whoso would enjoy high honor
> first must suitably display
> that he has been well schooled to such arts.

The culture of feudal times has left us nothing that shows more clearly than this text what the ruling class thought of itself, nor how fortune went about raising a man to such heights.

I T IS TIME for me to set the stage, in a few words, upon which these knights will perform their role. The theater is of course that of war, the interminable conflict of Capetians against Plantagenets. In 1066 the battle of Hastings had given England to William, duke of the Normans, and to the knights who followed him. The island had fallen under the domination of an aristocracy whose culture and whose every way of expressing that culture were Continenal, and which retained from the other side of the Channel, beyond the sepulcher of its ancestors, a good share of its interests, of its dominations and powers. Normandy belonged to the realm of France. It was not separated from it, and its duke remained attached to the Frankish sovereigns, successors of Charles the Bald and Hugh Capet, their vassal by the rites of homage, bound at the very least to do nothing that might harm them. But having become king himself by conquest, his actual power surpassed that of the other king his lord, whose perpetual concern was henceforth to diminish this inequality.

Yet, far from being attenuated, the disequilibrium was suddenly aggravated in the middle of the twelfth century, during William Marshal's childhood. The Norman kingdom had fallen to the husband of the Conqueror's granddaughter, another of the Capetian's grand vassals, Geoffrey Plantagenet, count of Anjou. His son Henry laid claim to the throne of England through his mother. He acceded to it in 1155, at the time he had just seized the wife of King Louis VII, Eleanor, thereby becoming count of Poitou and duke of Aquitaine. Thus his power extended over a good half of the kingdom of France, claimed to include Toulouse and the regions bounded by the Pyrenees, and in any case was uncontested north of the Loire; all its might was felt only a few leagues from Paris. This pressure upon the royal domains was intolerable. Therefore, tempered by the—highly effective—brake constituted by the ideology of royalty and the feudal bond, interrupted by prolonged truces because war could not then be waged for more than a few months at a time, the hostilities between Louis VII and Philip Augustus on the one hand, and on the other Henry II and his sons Richard Coeur de Lion and John Lackland, who succeeded him one after the other, were not to cease until the earl's death.

During the three-quarters of a century covered by the narrative I am using, a fissure gradually widened by the crossing over of the Anglo-Norman aristocracy: by degrees a part of this aristocracy became aware of being more solidly attached to England. Yet even after Normandy, Maine, Anjou were conquered by Philip Augustus, the king of England's knights did not cease feeling at home on the other side of the Channel, in close cultural solidarity with the knights of the king of France, sharing their scorn and their defiance of all who bore arms over the Loire, in Aquitaine.

No real battle occurred before Bouvines (1214) and Lincoln (1217), merely a series of skirmishes, punctuated on occasion by bursts of more intense aggression which constituted the very savor of chivalric existence. About the latter, by the turn of his phrases, the choice of his words, by the interaction of memory and forgetting, by what it avows and what it conceals, the life of William Marshal teaches us everything. And then the biography is here ready-made. With the help of those who have subjected it to the most learned scrutiny, Paul Meyer and Sidney Painter, I can let myself share with those who listened to it for the first time, nearly eight hundred years ago, the intense pleasure afforded by so splendid a text.

3

ACCORDING to the rules of that special literary genre constituted by saints' *Lives*, narrative must begin with the lineage that produced the hero as its finest flower. Such evocations of ancestry seemed indispensable, "for from a good tree comes good fruit," as our text repeats. Does not each man receive at birth, transmitted by the blood of his forebears, the seed of those virtues he must bring to blossom? This epoch regarded sanctity as atavistic, and valor as well. Therefore, William Marshal's *Life* begins with his lineage, but does not trace very far back; it stops at his father and one maternal uncle. As a matter of fact, this hero was a "new man" and made it a point of honor to owe none of his glory to others. We may assume that in his own lifetime he had seldom spoken of his all-too-obscure ancestors. Hence their memory was not venerated, once William was dead, by his son and his friends. Moreover, of all the honors and wordly possessions on which the dying earl's greatness was based in 1219, the share that had come to him from his forebears might seem paltry enough; hence, no extended genealogy.

It is from another source, then—from the royal charter that conferred the office of marshal upon William late in his life—that we learn the name of his paternal grandfather, Gilbert. Yet this name suggests he was the son or nephew of one of the adventurers who followed the Conqueror or joined him in England, attracted by the lure of booty. Perhaps a younger son, this unknown knight surely came from the Continent. We may note that this origin was forgotten by the beginning of the thirteenth century, and in any case that no great issue was made of it among his descendants. William Marshal is accounted an Englishman; he feels himself to be English; he regards the Normans, the French *a fortiori*, as foreigners— which does not keep him from admiring French knights, granting them first rank "for their valor, and their worth, and the honor of their country."

A century before his grandson's death, this Gilbert had performed for Henry I of England the functions of marshal of the court; hence his surname, which would become the family name. At this period, marshals lived as domestics; clothed and fed like other members of the household, they expected, beyond their employer's largesse, certain additional benefits, which varied according to the rank they occupied in the hierarchy of servants. Marshals were not situated at the top of this ladder; they were subordinates of one of the major officers, the constable, who controlled the seigneurial stables and everything to do with the horses. But because the cavalry's role in military actions had continued to grow since the year 1000, the marshal's function had assumed greater distinction and greater political value. Its importance and fruitfulness was of course in direct proportion to the power of the masters served. In the "family" of the king of England, the marshal of the court, in Gilbert's day, governed the armed services owed by the vassals of the crown and the disbursement of all moneys earmarked for warfare; it was also incumbent upon him to maintain order in the sovereign's entourage. Custom, henceforth established in writing, set his wages: fourteen *deniers*, one half-septier of wine, and one candle a day, if he took his meals in the house with the rest; twenty-four *deniers*, one loaf of bread, one septier of wine, and twenty-four candle-ends, if he had to feed himself. In formal court sessions, when the king created an earl or a baron, the marshal was further entitled to one saddled palfrey for each new knight.

Such household offices soon became hereditary. On Gilbert's death around 1130, his oldest son, John—William's father—inherited the title and the prerogatives attached to it; he retained them after 1139, when he definitively left the court and the king's person. At this time the king was gradually losing his power. In 1135, Stephen of Blois had succeeded his uncle, Henry I, who had no legitimate son still alive. Stephen had not ascended the throne without difficulty; to gain acceptance, he was obliged to increase concessions to the nobles. He was besieged, in fact, by all those who, to justify their insubordination and to demand more privileges, proclaimed Matilda, the late king's daughter, a more direct heir than Stephen. Their number gradually increased, while the treasury gradually emptied. Disturbances beset the divided realm. In each province, old hatreds revived, old greeds, and the thirst for possessions at one's neighbor's expense. Some sided with the crowned king, some with the woman who disputed his succession. Such was the case around Marlborough Castle in Wiltshire, where John Marshal had retired to his own lands, regarding the occasion as a favorable one to pursue his own interests. This pursuit, in which, as the poem says, "one loses, the other wins," was war. By which we may understand pillage, rapine, and a hunt for spoils. From the other side of the plain, John encountered Patrick, guardian of Salisbury Castle, leader of a rival faction. Here we reach the extreme limits of family memory. In these mists of time, John's figure is scarcely discernible. It was recalled only that he gave with a full hand and that, being neither earl nor baron of great wealth, he yet managed to maintain a great troop of knights —three hundred, the text says, doubtless exaggerating. At least two events remain more clearly inscribed in memory, two facts of very great consequence, as it happens: both are at the root of the great good fortune by which William was to be favored. I regard them as the source of all his future success.

First of all, John Marshal happened to make the right

choice at the right time: he sided with Matilda. During an excursion she was making in the vicinity of his lands, John served Matilda at the peril of his own life. One day when her little troop was giving way before the king's superior forces, John covered her retreat. Here we may note one of those specific details—infinitesimal but arresting, as this one proved to be for these impassioned knights—that frequently resist oblivion when it tears the web of memory. Escape was essential, and had to be instantaneous. Matilda, like all women in those days, rode sidesaddle; this was delaying their progress. "Lady, I swear to you by Jesus Christ," John apparently told her, "you cannot spur your horse in that posture. You must take one leg and put it over the saddle-bow." He himself held fast, falling back to the convent of Wherwhell, where he sought to engage the pursuers, at least momentarily. The enemy set fire to the tower in which he had taken refuge; the melting lead of the roof dripped upon his face; the king's men left him for dead. God be thanked, he escaped. He was seen returning on foot to Marlborough, but with only one eye. The memory of princes is short, yet Matilda recalled the exploit, the devotion that inspired it, nor did her son, Henry Plantagenet, forget it when, upon Stephen's death in 1154, he became king of England. Thus John had won the love and favor of the patron from whom there was the most to gain.

He gradually advanced himself by his valor, and made a further gain by marrying the daughter of a great house. From the start of this story, we can see the decisive effects that matrimonial strategies had on movements of social advancement in this period and in this milieu. Like all firstborn sons, John Marshal had been married early; his wife, about whom we know nothing, since for William and for his biographer she was of no use whatever, had borne him two sons. Now an opportunity appeared to contract a much more profitable alliance. It became evident that Matilda would prevail; Patrick, John's rival, ranged himself with the probable victors.

In the little local war, he had the upper hand; moreover, as no one in William's entourage denied fifty years later, he was of much nobler blood than John and possessed greater power. He offered his allegiance for a price. In order to win him over, the Plantagenets made him earl of Salisbury. In return they persuaded him to marry his sister to John, their loyal supporter. This was one function that marriages served: to reconcile enemies, to consolidate peace. Without hesitating—such substitutions of wives were then common currency—John repudiated his wife and took the new one, acting, the panegyric tells us, out of what we should call civic interest and in order to please his lord; to settle the dispute between him and Patrick, and not out of greed. We need not swallow all of what Jean le Trouvère tells us on this point: the second wife, the damsel Sibylla, was in fact worth a great deal more to John than the first.

S HE WAS William's mother, William being the second of the four sons, as well as two daughters, whom John Marshal engendered "upon her." Hence he took fourth place among the eventual heirs, preceded by the sons from the first marriage, Gilbert and Walter (about whom we know that Walter, at least, held the office of marshal after his father), then by John, his older brother, who bore his father's name and who succeeded him in his turn. In this wealth of male progeny, William thus figured among the supernumeraries, with Anselm, who followed him, and last of all Henry. This youngest son was placed in the Church; his brother's success afforded him, after a long wait, a great advance: he died bishop of Exeter. What value did the household place on these boys, whose misfortune was not to be born first? An anecdote—wherein the hero makes his entrance at perhaps the age of five or six, and was to describe the incident as one of his earliest memories—sheds some light on the condition of children in knightly society. Of this condition we learn virtually nothing from the documents we possess, and we are so ill-informed that many historians, myself included, are inclined to believe that the knights' sons—aside from the firstborn, and even then—were of no interest to their fathers until they were of an age to fight at their side, or against them. Let us consider the episode more closely.

It occurred during the conflict between John Marshal and King Stephen, who was laying siege to the town of Newbury. Impatient, enraged, swearing to take vengeance on the wretches who had the impudence to resist him so long— indeed, the leader of the garrison refused to surrender the castle, and the foot soldiers dared repel the assaults of his knights—the king persisted in the siege, though he was obliged eventually to come to terms. The feudal combat was interrupted by one truce after another; once the action lost its cutting edge, the small bands of soldiers disintegrated—out of boredom; when the siege was an extended one, the knights were observed to slip away one after the other. Then the leaders were obliged to speak, to agree to a mutual re- spite in order to regroup their forces, then to resume hostili- ties for a new, brief effort. Hence a one-day truce was agreed upon for the defenders of Newbury, then a longer truce for their supporter, John Marshal, who had promised to per- suade Matilda to surrender the stronghold. Yet Stephen sought guarantees, demanding that he be given one of John's sons as a hostage. William, the fourth son, was chosen. A poor precaution, as it turned out. It did not keep John from resupplying the castle during the brief truce. The king real- ized that he had been flouted. The son, according to the text, thereby found himself "at risk," or as we should say, in danger. Then came forward the *losengiers*, who are always poor advisers, caitiffs who engaged to hang William, or at least threatened to do as much. Informed, the father let it be known that the boy's life mattered little to him: he still pos- sessed "the hammer and the forge to produce another such, even finer."

What are we to make of such a boast? That fathers were so prolific and infant mortality so ruinous that they were quite unconcerned for their offspring, even for the males? Or rather that such a response belongs to the standard libretto of that grand opera being performed—splendid vociferations, splendid gestures—on the stage of feudal warfare, where what mattered, as much as any exchange of blows, was to intimidate, to frighten, to convince the adversary by words and dumb show? I am personally convinced that no one on either side believed that anyone would go all the way, to the point of capital execution. We see this clearly when, after this reply, the spectacle continues in a series of suspensions. Of course in England, a more "primitive" country than the Continent, there was more cruelty. But among those interested in reading, at the beginning of the thirteenth century, the history of William Marshal, who could suppose—save in the perspective of a century, a past that had become legendary—that anyone actually intended to sacrifice a hostage, and furthermore the son of a man of quality, and dangerous as well? The interest of this performance, which perhaps existed only in the family mythology and whose memory, in any case, was greatly embellished, abides, as far as I can see, in the sentiments attributed to one of the two leading players: King Stephen.

He is shown to us moved by a little child. Doubtless this sovereign's actions and the memory cherished of them, the place that was made for Henry II's predecessor in the gallery of royal portraits, tended to give him the features of a weak man, feminine attributes, a rather foolish soft-heartedness. But even so? William's biographer describes the king as melting, "gentleness" overflowing his heart, taking the child in his arms and upbraiding the *losengiers,* because the boy wanted to play with the javelin of a knight escorting him to the gallows, then because he wanted to swing on the catapult by which he was supposedly to be projected over the walls, and because he kept asking what the game was while both assailants and defenders strove to make the preparations for his supposed execution even more terrifying . . . William Marshal, summoning up his earliest memories, also said that in the course of the same siege and while he remained a hostage, the king delighted to keep him in his own tent, where the two of them played together on the flower-strewn floor, enjoying games of skill and chance—all of which the child won, of course. Such scenes nicely illustrate the earl's *chanson de geste;* it was appropriate that he be placed, upon his first appearance, in the arms of a king, in a situation heralding his future rise toward sovereign power. Did the tales seem unlikely to those who heard them told? Did such tender relationships cause surprise? Are we to exclude from the attitudes natural to these warriors an affection for little boys?

One feature of the child's condition is assured, at least, one on which William's entire fate depended: knights' sons, in this period, left the paternal household early; they would fulfill their apprenticeship to life elsewhere, those who were not the firstborn leaving the household—barring a lucky accident—forever. By the age of eight or ten, they were thus separated from their mother, from their sisters, from the women of their blood among whom they had hitherto lived and who were fond of them. We note, in fact, that it was his mother and his sisters that little William, as a hostage, first asked about from the household servant sent for news, when he saw the man peering into the royal tent. A break. A double break—with the house in which the child was born, with the feminine universe of the nursery. And an extremely abrupt transfer to another world, that of cavalcades, of stables, of armories, of hunts, of ambushes and manly sports. Here the boys grew up, members of the troop of horsemen, youths mingled with grown men in military promiscuity. They already belonged, in their subaltern position, sharing the circumstances of servants, to the group maintained in his house by another master, responsible for educating them, diverting them, who thereby became their new father, while the figure of the father—of the real father, the "natural" father—rapidly faded from their memory, since as younger sons they did not expect eventually to inherit from him.

Let us note that William Marshal seems to have totally expunged his father from his memory. That father died in 1165. We know of the event, and its date, but by other evidence, for the poem does not make the slightest allusion to his demise. Of course, William was far away; he was living at the time in Normandy. But he was an adult—nearly twenty years old. In this sort of memoir he has left, there is no concern to recall whether he was moved by the death of a man he had certainly not seen for many years, nor whether he desired to see him once more on his deathbed and escort him to his grave. We may wonder if he had not even forgotten where his father's remains were laid, and if he ever prayed for him. The only mourning he ever displayed, according to this memoir, followed the death of his older brother. When he heard of this, he demonstrated the requisite grief so strongly that those present supposed they saw "his heart break." He himself saw to the honors of these obsequies and sent his own knights to Marlborough to seek out the body, to accompany it and the widow with great pomp to Cirencester, where he himself joined them in three days. He ordered an extremely sumptuous service in that abbey of regular canons; here he very nearly fainted away— the only swoon for which a warrior could not be reproached. In truth, he was in great haste to return from these ceremonies: Richard Coeur de Lion—this was in 1194—was returning from captivity. William had heard the news at the same time that he learned of his brother's death, and the tidings, the poem tells us, had already acted as a balm to his soul. There was no time to be lost; he set off at a gallop to join the king, letting the funeral procession make its way without him to Bradenstoke where, the story has it, his "ancestors" lay.

His father? Certainly not. His maternal ancestors. The priory, as we know from its archives, had enjoyed the favors of Patrick of Salisbury, and it was on this side, the side of most honorable lineage to which he knew he owed most, that John Marshal II had chosen to be buried. Apparent indifference to the father's death, demonstrations of grief and of family piety at the older brother's death: these two attitudes are understandable. In 1165, William did not inherit—any more than in 1219 his own younger sons inherited, nor have we any evidence that they attended his funeral. In 1194, he inherited: John Marshal II had no sons. A new and formal proof of this feature of society: what was ritual in the manifestations of affection within the relationship, the external signs of attachment that are all we have as evidence—since we cannot see into their hearts, judge their sincere feelings —depended directly on the situation of those involved in the chain of succession. It is by the transmission of goods that this society strengthened the only affective links that had to be publicly expressed. One loved openly that relative who still possessed the rights one would take up when they fell from his dying hands, just as the vassal openly loves the lord from whom he has received largesse. William's father was mourned, his obsequies arranged, his memory served by Walter, the surviving son of the first two, who doubtless had returned to him once his apprenticeship was completed, and who was made marshal after him, and who died almost immediately thereafter. If William did not mourn his father, it is not that he reproached him for having sent him out of the house virtually empty-handed. His father had acted no differently from the way he himself was to behave with regard to his own youngest son, whom he greatly loved, as he says in his own words. He did not mourn him because he owed him nothing, except for having—without great pains, and perhaps without great pleasure either—engendered him and placed him in a good household to learn the proper use of arms and to arrive at a condition to make his own fortune.

W HEN PEACE is restored, Stephen dead, and Henry II crowned, young William thereupon takes leave of his mother, of his (weeping) sisters, and departs in very simple state, accompanied by no more than one "little fellow" like himself and one servant. He crosses the Channel. His father has decided to place his fourth son in Normandy with William of Tancarville, chamberlain of the king of England. This man is his first cousin, he holds a powerful castle and musters ninety-four knights under his banner, he is in a fine situation in the king's household: he is one of the most powerful of the close relatives. He is thereby obliged to "love" his lineage more than others, to "ennoble" it as much as he can, to "honor" it. He is implicitly trusted in the relationship —the king counts on him. Hence he sees hordes of youths coming to him. It has been decided that these are not to be churchmen. Once it seems proper to take them from their mothers, they will be entrusted to him, to be treated as his "nephews," that is, as his grandsons. They are not his descendants, but the same blood as his flows in their veins. By virtue of the laws of a genetics commonly allowed in the nobility, they are therefore destined, if he will deign to cultivate their talents, to become as rich, as generous, as courageous as he is himself. He is glad to welcome these boys. The storerooms of the house are full. What better use could he make of these reserves of food, of all that wheat his vassals carry to his house, than to devote them to the growth of these young men? He raises them. By this function, as he knows, he takes their father's place, thereby multiplying his own progeniture well beyond what he himself could have engendered from his successive wives. He takes under his wing a troop of future warriors. They will be his forever, caught in the nets of deferential friendship whose captive judges that there is no more certain wealth in the world. The sire of

Tancarville rejoices to see these youths vie with one another in order to please him.

No sooner has he entered into this competition for his foster-father's love than William becomes an object of envy. His rivals keep saying to their master, Why burden yourself with this good-for-nothing, this "wastrel," who when he's not eating is asleep? The master pays no attention. William continues to eat well; his are "the finest pieces that leave the pot, even before they go to the lord's plate." The lord loves him, and he prospers. Soon he is a squire, following the warriors in their train and serving them. He remains in this preparatory condition eight years. William of Tancarville finally decides—his protégé is over twenty—to grant him his sword: a tool, but more, an emblem of the right and duty to do battle. This entrance into chivalry probably occurred in the spring of 1167. The *chanson de geste* gives no date, does not describe the ceremony. Which is a little surprising, for this day when childhood ends, when the grown man is admitted into adult society, is generally regarded as a crucial one; on this day, real life begins, and each knight remembers it as the finest of his existence. In the biography of the heir to the counts of Guînes, which was inserted in a genealogical chronicle some thirty years before the history of William Marshal was written, the date of such dubbing is the only specific chronological reference. Now, with regard to his own dubbing, William shared this reverence. More pious than the biographer suggests, he preserved the feeling of having been, by this liturgy, steeped for the rest of his days in divine grace. In 1189, to his friends who feared for his life, or at least for his fortune at a decisive moment, he apparently said, "God, may He be thanked for it, has since I am a knight done me great good all my days; my courage now rests upon the certainty that He will continue." In his mind, chivalry, the source of grace and favor, was indeed what the theologians of the time defined as a sacrament. Then why such discretion about the rite itself? The best hypothesis I can make is as follows: for the younger son, one goes to no great expense. He became a knight in a contingent, as was the custom in the great houses, but not in the first rank; in the general run, in the course of a routine ceremony.

However, the poem's author, citing the uncertainties of memory with regard to such remote times, has sought to magnify this crucial point in the biography of a hero whom he chiefly displays as a paragon of chivalry. Of the usual rite occurring after the sword was bestowed, of that sort of fantasia, the quintain—a knightly exercise when all the new knights charge a dummy's lance to give proof of their skill—Jean le Trouvère has made an actual battle. He reuses in this part of his narrative fragments of memories not securely attached to that engagement in which William had taken part, but five years later, at Neufchâtel-en-Bray. He was fighting here in the Norman camp to defend the count of Eu against attack by the Flemish, men from Ponthieu and Boulogne. In this context, in the heart of this tumultous, violent, desperate engagement—as all such clashes were, in the course of pillaging expeditions, but which Jean makes as spectacular as a tourney, and the word "tourney" comes to his pen quite spontaneously—he locates the requisite ordeal of the young man who has just taken his place among the warriors and who here, before a numerous public (uniting representatives of both sexes and of various levels of society: knights, ladies, damsels, bourgeois), will demonstrate that he is worthy of them. "Herein did he give proof of his valor," the text says. And therein showed such virtue that the onlookers "could not believe he was still a newcomer to feats of arms." No one, we are told, expected him to reveal himself so fully. At the beginning of the affair, he was prepared to take his place beside the chamberlain, who sent away this tyro: "William, stand back, be not so eager. Let the knights pass first." Whereas, being a knight himself, he believed his place was to the fore. As he proved it was: risking his life, not riding at dummies but at the most dangerous combatants —those knights called *sergeants* to distinguish them from those of better birth and who, for their part, did not hesitate to strike hard. They rushed against him, brandishing ignoble weapons, those iron hooks which in Flanders serve to pull down the houses of bourgeois disloyal to their promises of peace. They caught him by the shoulder, seeking to throw him from his mount. He held fast. Thirteen iron links of his chain-mail shirt gave way, but he did not fall off the horse he had just received with his sword, a horse worth a great deal, which he did not hesitate to risk with himself and which, less well protected then the armored rider, was fatally wounded. Nothing in common here with the quintain jousts.

That evening, as was customary at the conclusion of the dubbings, the chamberlain held his court. There was great and fine feasting: "splendid viands bought with good coin," victuals sold by the merchants and of finer quality than what is taken from the salting tubs of the house. Eighty knights are to satisfy their hunger: to feed one's men in abundance is the duty of the good lord and master. His intimates also expect that he entertain them. When one has eaten, one talks. Tales are told of the fine feats of the day; "rich words and fine sayings." Jokes. William of Mandeville, a baron, seeks to raise a laugh in his turn: "Marshal, give me a gift, for friendship's sake." "What gift?" "A crupper or some old harness." Naive, the new knight protests he has nothing left; "he did not seek to gain possessions, but to deliver the town." He has lost everything. The table laughs, and he understands the lesson: he has his valor to sell. He learns thus that the first use of valor is to make a knight rich. Now for the moment, after the feasting, after having galloped, having fought, having drunk, eaten and spoken better than was ever done in the most sumptuous dubbings of Pentecost, he finds himself in the greatest poverty of his entire life. This is the low-water mark, the nadir of his existence.

Indeed, as soon as the troop was back at Tancarville, the chamberlain announced to the new knights that they were no longer to count on anything but themselves. Their apprenticeship over, he would no longer feed them. Let them take to the land, let them go, says the text, "turning about the world." Turning—the word is significant. Endlessly on the move and never in a straight line, never making for a goal: there is no goal. Searching here and there. Questing. Quest, conquest, "to win one's worth," all alone. And for the first time. For during the previous break, when William had been obliged to leave his mother and sisters with a heavy heart, he was simply changing households; expelled, according to custom, from his father's house, he had made his way, armed—in a small way, to be sure, but his hands were not entirely empty—toward another house where custom saw to it that he was welcomed. This first departure was not a risk. Nor a liberation. Under the power of a new foster-father, his childhood was to continue. Today, it is truly ended. His sword girded on, William has become a man among men. He belongs to no one now but God. At the same time as the military baldric, he has received a power that is first of all a power over himself. The rites of dubbing consecrate this self-possession. We grasp their meaning; we understand that dubbing was of such importance in this society into which the poem introduces us that it was considered the main event of all masculine existence. Before receiving their weapons, the young men stripped themselves naked and washed their bodies—as one washed the body of the newborn and of the deceased. For this entrance, this passage, was analogous to those others, to birth and to death. It was as if these men had come into the world a second time—and the only time, in truth, that truly counted. Hitherto, their gestation had indeed been occurring under cover; they had remained at nurse, as it were, under guardianship. With errantry began freedom, but also danger. William, we are told by Jean, was then "in very great dread."

For William was not an eldest son. When the heir, the future head of the family, was dubbed a knight, custom required that he too be sent "turning," but in glory. His turn would be for show—to display everywhere, for months, sometimes for years, the honor of the house. The young man was exposed to dangers, of course, but he was supplied, without thought of expense, with what was necessary to face the ordeal with every likelihood of triumph, of showing himself off, of uniting generosity with prowess. For he had to be magnificent. Thus he departed escorted by companions, servitors, all in full panoply, and with many pieces of silver in his saddlebags. A younger son, William entered upon life without anything. Of what he had ritually received from his master at the same time as knighthood, he retained no more than his sword, his torn shirt of mail, his scar, the mark of the iron hook which he was to keep all his life long. His charger had died under him. As for his cloak, he was obliged to sell it for twenty-two Angevin *deniers*. This was little, ten times less than the price of a suitable war-horse, just enough to buy himself an ass to bear him and his arms: he could not, after all, set out on foot, his accouterments on his back.

For he was setting out to fight. To turn also meant to tourney. To proceed from one tournament to the next. To excel there, of course, like the firstborn sons, but not, like them, by throwing money from the windows. On the contrary, to win. To win his worth—and above all his living. To make his life. He had no sooner left the Tancarville household than he was already tourneying and winning. Indeed, when he was shown the door, when he was enjoined to take up errantry, news came of a tourney that was about to begin. William the chamberlain, who did not want to miss such an occasion, was in haste to form his "team." His former squire, a new knight, had not yet set out. He engaged him, as he might have engaged any passing horseman—in addition to the domestic squadron—in order to give him his opportunity, nothing more. The earl later liked to say that his master the

chamberlain had treated him as a friend, as his "nephew"—
the love of Charlemagne for Roland. But he also told how on
that decisive day—this was the first blow, the real one—he
had received from the chamberlain no more than "petty favors." He emphasized such parsimony to make it clear that
on the threshold of real life, he had been reduced to his own
means. In particular he wanted to convince the world that
entirely by his own means had he acquired the charger without which he could not have followed the others in their
profitable skirmishes. Since he no longer belonged to the
household, he had not participated in the distribution of
good mounts from the stables. One remained, however, in
the courtyard, a horse no one wanted any part of; though
fine and strong, it remained refractory to the reins, ill-trained
and too restive for anyone to dream of using it in any sportive
encounter. William leaped into the saddle, spurred it on,
mastered it in the course of a rodeo whose phases and feints
the poem describes in minute detail. He was then able to use
the horse so skillfully that upon that very day he took four
and a half prisoners (as it happened, he naively consented to
share the fifth with one of his companions, who declared he
had helped him to capture the man). This success permitted
him to complete his accouterment, to present himself in finer
fettle at the next tournament. Riding very well this time too,
but alone: ill or ill-advised, his master had not come. William
performed, he tells us, wondrously. On his own hook.

Already he was being talked of. And men were beginning
to envy him. Was he, at twenty or twenty-two, about to take
his own way? No knight, at this time, functioned independ-
ently for long. Each year, in the springtime, hundreds of
young men found themselves thus expelled from the nests
of the nobility, like a yeast of turbulence. Society protected
itself; by channeling this tide of youth, it immediately sequestered a disturbing impetuosity. The society I am observ-
ing was indeed friable; irresistibly, individuals were
constrained to join together, to combine into groups, and it

was still shoulder to shoulder, surrounded by friends, that each one advanced into life. A solitary knight-errantry existed only in fiction, and even there it was merely episodic. Solitude was experienced, not as a deliverance, but quite the contrary as a painful crisis, a kind of mortifying penance. The court awaits the return of every Lancelot, and the knights of legend dream during the ordeal, like Erec, of returning soon to the nest, or else, if they are not established, of settling down soon in a reassuring domestic conviviality. In reality, the warriors shuddered at the thought of remaining alone; isolation covered them with shame. The knight whom we see riding without company cut a wretched figure, a man dishonored or banished, like William when, suspected of adultery, he failed to clear himself and was obliged to flee, raging inwardly, at Christmastime, from the court at Caen. Fifteen years before, following his dubbing, it had been all he could do to separate himself from the chamberlain's household. When he had dared set out alone for his second tournament, he had astonished everyone. "Who is this knight, so skilled at the use he makes of his weapons?" asked sire Barnaby de Rougé. He was reassured; this horseman could be identified, located in a *formation*: "his shield is of Tancarville." William had indeed kept upon him the sign of the family where he had been trained, which had made him a man. He displayed it like a warrant, a patent of quality. But also as a safety-catch, a mark of belonging, a recourse against disfavor and perhaps ill-treatment, of which any man who appeared to be without comrades was regularly the object. And when he finally broke the link, it was to forge himself another one very quickly. He made haste to place himself under other colors, under a new patronage.

When I consult this invaluable document in order to follow the trajectory of a personal ascent—in order to construct from this example better hypotheses as to what might be the capillary movements of promotion in Western aristocracy during this half-century framing the year 1200 (that is in the spate of growth then sweeping Europe in the upswing of a prodigious development which, with the same energy, brought about the acceleration of monetary circulation, the strengthening of state structures, and consequently the multiplication of the individual's opportunities for advancement), one fact seems clear to me: the wheel of fortune, raising some, casting others down, turned ever faster in those days, even in this apparently stable social milieu constructed on its lineal armatures. Nonetheless, among the knights its movement seems a double one, functioning on superimposed levels. Below, a certain individual is borne along, rises, outstrips the rest, but within each social cell, at the heart of each household molecule under the master's very eyes, in a climate of harsh and permanent internal rivalry, one that sharpens envy, nourishes conspiracy and treachery. Meanwhile up above, and this time under the eyes of the masters of those principalities that constantly reinforce each other, a similar movement brings about the rise of certain houses. Hence the ambitious man must first of all triumph within his own group. But he who seeks to rise higher must take care to operate within the group closest to the source of largesse, best placed in relation to the eminent powers that are now those of the sovereigns.

Ceasing to be "retained"—to be a retainer—in the powerful family of his father's cousin, the sire of Tancarville, William now makes his unfettered way toward a still more powerful family, one that deigns to accept him as he is, having proved his worth, though without any possessions but his arms. This family was an inevitable choice: that of Patrick of Salisbury, his mother's brother. The arrangement of family relationships in knightly society attributed to the maternal uncle certain rights and duties with regard to his nephews. The line of which he was the head had already given a daughter to another household—he had lost his power over her, but this power, on the other hand, he meant to preserve over the children she would bring into the world. The uncle expected his sister's sons to love him better than their own father, and he himself felt called upon to love them more than the latter. Notably, to help them in their career. Now in most cases, this man was in a better position to do so, since by the effect of matrimonial strategies the wife was usually of higher birth than her husband. In order to make their way in the world, the boys consequently "turned" in the direction of their maternal ancestry. When they had been dedicated to the service of God, they rose within the ecclesiastical ranks thanks to the uncle who was a canon, abbot, or bishop; when they were knights, they set out to do battle in the troops of the uncle who was a knight-banneret, certain of finding in his entourage a firm support, a warm friendship, and the most assured opportunities of making their fortune.

William made this choice. In the days that followed his dubbing and his very first combats, he passed back over the Channel. He wanted, he said, to visit his "good lineage"— by which we may understand the side where he felt he could count on the greatest profit. Taking leave, he received a last piece of advice from the sire of Tancarville: not to linger in England; the country was worthless for a man seeking to advance himself by the profession of arms. This was the word of a Norman, and distinctly prejudiced. Yet there was some truth in it, and young William took it for what it was worth. He had just learned what kind of profit could be won from the tournaments; he deduced that, for the time being, such tournaments were not being held on the other side of the Channel. At least in England—and this was the reason for the journey—he knew he could find a wealthier household. Over William of Tancarville, Patrick of Salisbury had the advantage of being an earl. In other words, he was placed immediately beneath the sovereign, at the highest degree of the hierarchy of honors and powers. Further, he was in favor at court. Ever since he had sided with the mother of King

Henry II, Patrick had been able to keep the Plantagenet's affection. Through him, his nephew approached a little closer to the royal house.

Hence it was in the king's service that, no sooner arrived, William returned to the Continent forthwith; this time he sailed for Poitou. Eleanor of Aquitaine, countess of Poitiers and queen of England, was on her way there to attempt to subdue her rebellious vassals. King Henry had chosen Patrick to guard his wife during the journey. While performing this protective function, the earl of Salisbury was attacked by one of the great rebel barons, the sire de Lusignan. Having first sequestered the queen, Patrick then turned to face his attackers, though insufficiently armed. To stop them, he had ridden ahead bareback. And while he was waiting for the better mount that his squires were bringing up, he was struck dead from behind, in the Poitevin way: it was everywhere said north of the Loire that the people of this country, as faithless as they were lawless, always behaved treacherously. This attack caused a scandal and was everywhere denounced as a crime on two counts: the ethic of true, noble, Frankish warriors ordained that knights were not to be killed, and in any case forbade killing them in this fashion, from behind, when they were not fully armed. Further and above all, the feudal ethic condemned the vassal who laid hands on his lord or on the one—Patrick, in this case—who was taking his place. Now it so happened that William avenged this odious crime, and I regard this exploit as decisive for his advancement.

Once he perceived the blow from which his uncle was dying, he acted according to the precepts of a third ethic, the most compelling of all, that of lineage. His relative, and this particular relative—his maternal uncle, his more than father —had fallen under the blows of a murderer. His duty was to leap to the rescue, to attempt to save the victim, or at least to wash away the offense in the assassin's blood. Boldly he dashed forward, bareheaded, without helmet. Soon there were sixty-eight against him, armed with pikes; bravely he managed to kill six of their horses; but finally, passing through the hedge where the young knight had taken up position, an adversary, once again from behind, pierced his thigh. He fell and was carried off, a splendid prize, grievously wounded. (Here occurs the episode of the lady with the linen cloth.) Of this brilliant feat of arms the echo was quite different from that of his tournament prowess. William was not jousting, nor was he seeking glory or booty. He was performing his duty, the first duty of a young man, opposing evil, truly risking his life. This alone might have been enough to give luster to his precocious fame. But it happened that the man whom he sought to avenge was the king's lieutenant. He therefore passed for having avenged the king himself and for having protected the queen, since in this business it was with the latter's person that the criminals were concerned. Eleanor was convinced of it: she gave hostages in exchange for William, released him from captivity, and took him among her own people. He was fed and armed by her. This fortuitous event transferred him from his uncle's intimacy to that of the sovereign.

THE MONARCHIC state had by now sufficiently cleared away the feudal underbrush to assume a certain maturity: to acquire the king's esteem only a few months after his dubbing determined a knight's career. Two years later, in the summer of 1170, Henry II constituted the household of his elder son, young Henry, whom he had just had anointed and crowned king. In the service of this prince, a boy of fifteen and therefore in his majority a year since according to the customs of the period, but who was not yet dubbed a knight, who still needed to be guided and protected, a man of trust was required who might be the heir-apparent's mentor, his instructor in the military arts, who might help him, even taking his place in difficult passes in order not to tarnish the glory of the house. Henry the father sought such a person among the young knights who had come to some eminence around him; it was William whom he designated to guard and to instruct the young king of England."

At twenty-five, then, William was appointed to a position well above his first hopes, member of the household, of the *mesnie*, as it was called, of the *hôtel* of young Henry. This body was formed of a tight, permanent nucleus of five or six knights (of whom William was one); on certain days it increased, sometimes to excess; it actually numbered two hundred knights on several occasions; ordinarily, the forces were about twenty warriors, among whom the Normans were the most numerous. Incontestably, William was the leader of the band, "outstripping all those of the *hôtel*." We might be justified in wondering if the biographer does not here assign the hero too prominent a role. Yet his testimony is confirmed by archival documents: in the list of the persons who subscribed to Henry's actions, the name of Marshal precedes those of all the ordinary knights; it comes immediately after the names of the first-category nobles, the barons. Let us envision William, then, as a kind of palace mayor; he keeps guard over his still-adolescent master, he directs him, he controls him. All his life William prided himself on having been, during those years, "sire and master of his lord" (and his biographer, following him, justifies: "By God, he might well have been, since he feasted him on high deeds"). Let us understand the meaning of the expression: Henry the Younger was in effect William's "lord" and William, like any vassal, owed him loyalty. Yet Henry regarded him as his own "master" in the pedagogic sense of this word: his master-at-arms. From this power proceeded the authority that made William the "sire" of this boy, his lord. In Latin, the suitable word would be *dominus*. William, strictly speaking, dominated young Henry. Now the latter was a king—associated with his father for the moment, and in a subaltern position. But Henry the Elder was nearing fifty, the age when princes died in those days. Henry the Younger would therefore not be junior much longer: he would be reigning alone. Then William would be of all men best placed to conquer fortune at his side.

For the time being, he educates young Henry, teaches him what the "valet," the little fellow, must gradually learn. This training continues at the heart of the squadron constituted by the *mesnie*, that vagabond horde which is "errant." Errantry and expenditure, the two necessarily go together. Now the young king possesses nothing of his own. He is taught to covet one of the great fiefs of his ancestors, Normandy, or Anjou. King Henry II, who mistrusts his immature son, is reluctant to put such splendid holdings in his hands. Consequently, the heir-apparent must continue to live off his father, who soon complains of his profligacy. Jealous men surround him, who spur him on: "Only the day before yesterday, it was five hundred *livres*. Not one of which is left him. On some other day, I know not which, he was given even a thousand . . . " While on their side the knights of the household encourage their leader to ever higher demands. All the noble lines of the period, except perhaps for that of the kings of France, were riven by the effects of this false situation: a young prince to whom everything will fall due, who is envied by his uncles and brothers, who is growing up and no longer tolerates a dependence on the generosity of his father . . . Impatience on both sides; "many bitter words of high feeling"; inexorably the discord sharpens, and all those who have an interest in the aggravation of these domestic quarrels, especially the leaders of the adverse seigneuries, busy themselves poisoning the dispute, driving the old and the young man against each other. In the Plantagenet house, the rupture finally comes about. In 1173, while a good proportion of the barony had risen in England against the expansion of state power, Henry II, holding court at Alençon, learned that his elder son had risen in revolt, taking Richard, his brother with him. Established south of the Loire, on lands belonging to their mother, they were joined by all the aristocracy of Aquitaine, in a state of permanent rebellion and merely seeking such an occasion. The king of France, of course, supported them, his policy being to take advantage of whatever might weaken his great rival. William sided with his immediate lord. This was his duty: he was of his "family" and was "his man"; he belonged to him. But he was also considering his own interests: he was counting on the future, on youth, on what he regarded as the imminent promotion of the young man whose "sire" he was. The chronicler Benedict of Peterborough, when he relates the dispute, inscribes William Marshal on the list of those who betrayed Henry II.

The other Henry, young Henry, was then nineteen years old. He, too, was a king but had no sword, for he had not yet been dubbed a knight. And for the warriors of his house, this was a disgrace; they kept repeating: let him soon be dubbed, "his *mesnie* will be all the braver, more greatly honored, and most of all more joyous." As a matter of fact, Henry did not know his profession adequately, nor had he entirely grown into it. Moreover, his father was in no hurry. The author of the earl's story claims that the king hoped, in order to "raise up" his heir, to see him dubbed knight by the king of France. It was indeed frequently incumbent upon the father-in-law—which Louis VII had been since the wedding of 1171—to arm his son-in-law. We may nonetheless suppose that Jean le Trouvère says this to shed more luster on his hero. Actually, the military sacrament was not administered by an anointed king; it was administered by William Marshal, a poor knight who did not possess "an acre of ground, or anything else save his chivalry." His postulant advanced toward him, presenting the sword: "From God and from you, I would receive this honor." William girded him with the sword, then kissed the new knight. Swollen with glory and envied by all around him, especially the high lords of the court of France whom Louis VII had dispatched: one of his brothers, his constable, the sire de Montmorency, Guillaume des Barres. For the time being they were allies of the rebel son. They joined in friendship with William Marshal, at this time a friendship that was never to weaken, despite all conflicts and reversals of alliance: war at this time was quite as much as peace, a natural condition, a normal thing, an occupation, a way and a means of life; temporary and, for the knights, agreeable; it wrought no lasting effect upon the heart's bonds.

I wonder if, electing William his master, the new knight had not sought to demonstrate his independence in the midst of the rebellion, to avoid subjecting himself to one more powerful than he by that submission every knight owed to whoever had introduced him into his "order." I wonder if young Henry did not want his sponsor to be, as he himself said, God and God alone. And William, of course —but he was nothing. Yet William considered till his dying day that the greatest honor he had ever received was to have taken this role at so young an age. As a child he had played in the king of England's arms. Now with his own hands he was leading the king of England from childhood to full manhood. What might he not expect henceforth from his lord?

In autumn of 1174, peace returned, a very harsh peace for the English rebels. But the old king granted his son pardon, nor did he hold any grudges against William, who had not faltered in his loyalty: domestic fidelity then prevailed over all others, and William's duty was to serve it first. Young Henry was in no great hurry to return to his father—he lingered on the Continent. Finally, a year later, he crossed the Channel with his *hôtel*. He was soon bored: there were no tournaments in England, and he wearied of hunting, palavering, "sojourning" at his ease. "Long sojourns shame a young man"—which means, fill him with shame. Shamed, idle, the "young men," the "bachelors" are restless and make themselves intolerable. As young Henry did in a matter of months. As soon as he began to talk of making a pilgrimage to Saint James of Compostella, King Henry gladly granted him leave to go, agreeing, the sooner to be rid of him, to pay once again for an additional tournament. The young king and his men therefore rushed to the Continent, choosing the shortest way across the Channel, from Dover to Wissant, near Boulogne. The powerful count of Flanders, Philip of Alsace, who was elaborating an arrogant strategy in the kingdom of France, was waiting for the troop, intending to adopt and distract the neophyte at its head. On April 19, 1176, life regained its savor, and the country of tourneys and knight-errantry opened once again before the squadron that disembarked, William Marshal at their head.

4

ABOUT TO be thirty, William Marshal regarded himself, for the first time, as entirely his own master. Of course he remained a member of a group—it was he himself who held the reins, in both hands. After all, the titular leader of the company whose colors floated over him, the new knight William had just dubbed, as yet too inexperienced, could hardly do without him, and abided altogether by his aid and counsel. In fact, William had, like any baron, responsibility for a house, and a very independent one. How would he behave? How did he later describe how he had behaved, he who sought to be known as chivalry's finest flower?

His function, his duty to himself, to the lord he served and to all the men of the "family," consisted, to speak in the fashion of the *Histoire's* author, in *conquering worth*—translate *worth* as the renown of valor—and honor. To increase this honor, in any case to spare no pains to keep that honor from weakening, to avoid being shamed. Shame was what the men of this world feared might come to them chiefly through the misconduct of women, those of their immediate family, their own wives above all. Henry, youngest of all the knights, was the only married man in the band, not only because there were no other firstborn males among them but because these groups, these *mesnies*, were identified with noble houses built around a single conjugal pair. Hence it was incumbent upon the heir-apparent to the king of England to keep a close watch upon his spouse. But the other knights, William and his comrades, were bachelors. They ran fewer risks. Their ardor was entirely focused upon fulfilling the obligations of chivalry, upon respecting the rules of an ethic inculcated during adolescence and kept alive in their minds by all the stories and songs they listened to. Of this ethic, the chief constraints were of three kinds.

Loyalty first of all. To keep one's word, not to betray one's sworn faith. This requirement was gauged according to a strict hierarchical framework. The knight was situated at the center of several interlocking structures whose coherence was sustained by his loyalty. He had to be loyal to the members of all these structures. But in the face of contradictory requirements, he would be loyal first of all to those closest to him and chiefly to the man at the head of this initial body; more distant friends came next, the faith owed to them being flexible and yielding—though without breaking—in the presence of firmer kinds. If it would serve the head of the house, the direct and immediate master, then betraying his other friendships was not a fault. No one could take umbrage at such behavior. Benedict of Peterborough was wrong to tax William Marshal with treachery, and as we have seen, Henry II was not deluded as to William's behavior.

The second duty of these warriors was to conduct themselves as champions: feats of valor—to do battle and to triumph, but conforming to certain laws. The knight does not engage in combat as foot soldiers do. In 1197, at a turning point of the harsh war the Anglo-Norman troops were waging against the king of France, William remarked upon this one day to Count Baldwin of Flanders. Followed by the troop of his foot soldiers, the count offered to form a kind of enclosure with the victualers' carts. Here the sheltered knights would await the adversary's assault. William strongly opposed this plan. Rather let these carts be arranged so as to keep the enemy foot soldiers from intervening: let villeins face villeins. But for men whose function and honor it is to bear noble arms, no fortress; they will confront the enemy without "foxing" (eager to behave not like foxes but like lions), in open field, despising all ambush, in battle array, altogether exposed. The champion seeks no other protection than the expertise of his charger, the quality of his armor, and the devotion of comrades of his own rank whose friendship sustains him. Honor obliges him to appear intrepid, and to the point of folly. Of this temerity, William's companions were to complain—fraternally—before the walls of Montmirail, during the wars of Maine: he went too far. Over the moat around the stronghold to be taken, a single narrow donkey-back bridge had been thrown. On its crest were posted ten enemy soldiers, one mounted, all armed with pikes. William rode at a gallop against this obstacle; of its own accord, his horse turned round—had it deviated by an inch, his rider would have been cast over the side. Of such temerities the earl was later to boast. When he was instructing young Henry, he urged him to take risks of this kind without considering the danger, even rushing to his pupil's rescue in order to protect him from too fateful an encounter, thereby appropriating glory for himself.

Perhaps here I ought to insert a fourth precept: in quite as bold a manner, to win the love of women—of ladies. Following this principle afforded William the disappointments I have related. But women play so small a part in our narrative that I shall pass over *courtoisie* and confine myself to the third of the necessary virtues: *largesse*, or generosity. This is what truly makes the gentleman, establishes social distinction. The biography says so quite clearly: "*Gentillesse* [nobility] is nourished within the house of generosity." The knight owes it to himself to keep nothing in his hands. All that comes to him he gives away. From his generosity he derives his strength and the essentials of his power, in any case, all his renown and the warm friendship that surrounds him. The only praise William liked to hear of his father was that he had spread his riches in abundance; and it was doubtless primarily for his munificence, for his inability to keep anything back, for the conspicuous waste of which he was the overflowing source, distributing all his possessions in order to delight those he loved, that the hero of the *chanson de geste* sought to be admired.

But it is chiefly at this nucleus of its armatures that we see the knightly ethic in conflict with reality. It had been constructed at a time when currency had little circulation, when gift and countergift constituted almost everything which, in the movement of wealth, did not proceed from inheritance. Now, during the very sudden growth of the last quarter of the twelfth century, the invasion of currency has proceeded to overturn everything. It has become obvious to the least perspicacious that the leaders of the renascent states are "greasing palms," their policy furthered as much by money as by arms; it was by money that King Henry II could detach the French barons from his rebellious heir-apparent, by money that Philip Augustus later won the support of the papal curia. This new power of *deniers* is demoralizing. For currency—like seeking protection behind palisades—is the business of villeins, and contemptible. Villeins and bourgeois do not give—they love money too much, they accumulate it, make it fructify, and lend it out at usurious rates. Remember William's rage in the presence of the monk and his ravished "victim." Whereas the knight, according to the ethic of his order, touches money only with repugnance and to expend it forthwith in feasting. Yet nowadays the knight is obliged to use money for serious matters, and increasingly. Everything costs money. This is especially true of equipment indispensable to the warriors, accouterments quickly exhausted, notably the good horses on which a man's skill depends and which are lost in military sport, are crippled in charges, collapse under their riders. Each squad of knights-errant is thus surrounded by a host of eager merchants who follow it, precede it, await it, join it at each halt, gathering as soon as a significant engagement is in sight. They open their packs, display their wares, tempt their customers. They offer everything, but at a price. No one, therefore, can pursue glory and honor without flinging money away, and no longer for his own pleasure.

The young king's household, for example, is so extravagant that its creditors besiege it from daybreak, at the outset of each march. Then a knight discovers that he owes this one three hundred *livres*, that one a hundred, two hundred, for finery but also for palfreys, for victuals; on one day the debt "rises indeed to six hundred *livres*," admits the writer who keeps accounts. Who could find such sums in the coffers? Then William comes forward: "The *mesnie* has not these moneys, but you shall have them within a month," and his word is accepted. On one occasion, one of these rowdy commoners trying their luck in wild and desolate regions, Sancho, the leader of a party of mercenaries whom young Henry had taken on and who had not received their pay (commerce had indeed insinuated itself even into warfare: men were paid to wage it, and paid dear if they were specialists), put his hand on the bridle of the horse William was riding: "You are taken." "Why?" "So you may pay me the money I am owed; I shall release you for one hundred *marcs*." "I am a poor knight, I have nothing. But I pledge that I shall give myself up to your prison on the day as you shall set." Thus we see William taken prisoner for the debts of his lord. Luckily, he was able to find the sum and free himself. But there remains the embarrassment of these growing obligations, the disgust of having to bind oneself on one's word, to surrender oneself body and soul, to become the prisoner of merchants and commoners. And finally, this bitter discovery: "When possessions fail, pride must fall"; poverty too can cause shame. We note the constant obsession with shame. No longer to be able to sustain one's rank, to play one's part in the great game of chivalry, for lack of money! How to obtain it nobly, without demeaning oneself, when one is not going to inherit a single manor, when one does not have behind one those stewards who, without the master's taking the trouble, assure seigneurial rights? Henceforth money appears to be indispensable to honor at the very moment honor demands it be scorned, and this precisely at the moment when it is crucial to nourish that honor, to exalt it, when one is still a "young knight." Such is the agonizing dilemma that confronts William Marshal day after day upon his return to France, and during the next seven years, all given over to tournaments.

T HE INFATUATION with tournaments was then at its height. By the twenties of the thirteenth century, when our narrative was written, contemporaries apparently considered that it had already distinctly subsided. This at least is our author's point of view; we must not be too eager to take as a simple literary commonplace these lamentations over the disappearance of knightly prowess. Let us start with this fact: when Jean le Trouvère deals with the years 1173–1183, he speaks of virtually nothing but tournaments for over twenty-five hundred lines. No document, to my knowledge, informs us better as to what this sport then was. Like bullfights or soccer today, it was not practiced everywhere. A man living in England who wished to participate in the tournaments, as I have noted, was obliged to cross the Channel. William Marshal's biography contains the description of sixteen tournaments and locates all except one very precisely. Thus we perceive the paradise of the participants delimited by a line that runs through Fourgères, Auxerre, Épernay, Abbeville. We also see that only two of these tournaments were held in the very heart of the feudal principalities: at Pleurs near Sézanne, in the county of Champagne, and at Saint-Pierre-sur-Dives, near Caen, in the duchy of Normandy. That all the rest were organized on the borders, the "marches" of these political structures, on the site of the old forest frontiers that in ancient times separated the realms (at the limits of the Vermandois and the Capetian country, between Gournai and Resson, near Compiègne; three times on the edges of Champagne at Lagny and at Joigny, opposite the Ile-de-France and the duchy of Burgundy on the edges of Normandy, at Eu, opposite Ponthieu, at Saint-James and at Saint-Brice, opposite Brittany and Maine, at Anet, Maintenon, Épernon, opposite Le Perche and in the county of Blois). Such localization is suggestive to those who seek the origins of these simulacra of battle.

As for the participants, they came in part from the region circumscribed by the most eccentric of these fifteen sites, and which I regard as the mother province, but also in part from outside it. The space of recruitment thus broadly aureoled the space of the engagements. Many warriors came from England, and from farther still; one king of Scotland figured as a fascinated spectator. Many came from Brittany, from Anjou, from Poitou, but none from more southerly regions. Many came from Burgundy, from Flanders, from Hainaut, some from Thiais, from Aval, that is, from Basse-Lorraine; from beyond, from farther east, no one. Indeed, the vogue of a sport depends, as much as on tradition, on the ardor of those who organize it and spend lavishly for the success of its manifestations. In order to understand the geography of the tournaments, we must therefore consider their promoters.

No king figures among them except young Henry, who is, precisely, *young* and who, under his father's authority, plays the part of the prince of youth, delegated to frivolous activities, and whose royalty no one takes seriously. It did not seem decent that God's lieutenants, anointed by the ritual unction of a semireligious power, should participate in such entertainments that the Church in all its councils had condemned for half a century as a snare of the Devil; the tournaments, it claimed, diverted the knights of Christ from important military affairs, notably the crusade; they mutilated, weakened, and decimated these warriors dedicated to opposing evil, heresy, and unbelief. Indeed, there was greater risk of death in these sportive confrontations than in warfare. However, dukes and earls—the higher barons—did not feel closely bound by such ecclesiastical prohibitions; there were twenty of them at the Lagny tournament. We are tempted to see them as members of a kind of club, a society for the encouragement of tourneys. In any case we may consider some as controlling the business of the tournaments. They determined their proper distribution throughout the season and spread the necessary publicity. All chivalry counted on their office. To fill it properly was the most effective means of extending their prestige and the highest-prized, hence most profitable, way of deploying their *largesse* for the warm gratitude it won them from what was liveliest and most spirited in military society: those "young knights" who formed the great majority of the participants, since of all those who measured themselves in the lists, the "high barons" were virtually the only ones who were married. The ruling powers, throughout history, have endeavored to sustain themselves by organizing games and sports. I am convinced that the high nobility in the north of the kingdom of France, at the end of the twelfth century, found no surer trump card for resisting a growing royal authority than by winning over the knights with the offer of a favorite diversion. It was also for pleasure's sake that certain barons indulged themselves, and to the hilt, in what we might call a patronage: the counts of Clermont, of Beaumont, of Saint-Pol, of Boulogne; Robert of Dreux, Philip Augustus's first cousin; Thibaud of Blois; the duke of Burgundy; the count of Hainaut. One of the most enthusiastic at this time was Philip of Alsace; it was he who invited young Henry, as soon as he had disembarked, to participate; he was waiting for him at Arras to lead him at once to the Gournai tournament, taking just time enough to equip him splendidly at his own expense.

The author of the history of William Marshal apologizes: he cannot describe in detail the vicissitudes of all the tournaments. There were too many of them: "Almost every week, tournaments were held in one place or another." If authentic warfare came to a stop in bad weather—the French hated fighting, the narrative says, "when cold clasps the air" —the craving for such sport was so strong that neither cold nor inclemency interrupted the tournaments for long, though it was not a good idea to fight in heavy rain, above all since no one wanted to expose horses and armor to winter damp, especially the precious and fragile chain-mail garments that rusted so easily. At Gournai, one tourney took place in the very last days of November 1182; another followed it on January 13; the intermission was thus reduced to the briefest possible period, the brief fast imposed by Advent, the period of abstinence preceding Christmas, and, during the eight days after this holiday, the solemnities when the kings held court in all their glory, crowned and presiding over the great palavers (as Henry II did that very year at Caen). Similar interruptions occurred, and for the same reasons, around Easter, Pentecost, All Saints' Day. But outside of these few vacations, chivalry observed no recess.

Of course, not all its members participated in each encounter, but some of the tournaments attracted a very large crowd. At Lagny, incontestably the most successful of all tournaments evoked by our text, three thousand knights had entered, each accompanied by his servants. There also figured several companies of combatants of low birth, despised but nonetheless utilized, for such men were very skillful at wielding the base weapons, pikes and hooks, and these mercenary bands made on the occasion, as in real hostilities, a decisive contribution. Hence let us reckon the number at over ten thousand warriors and perhaps as many horses; let us also add the throng of parasites, horse-dealers, moneychangers, whores, all gathered in hopes of harvesting from this bellicose festivity more money than from the most popular pilgrimages. A mob. For two or three days near Lagny, a town famous for its fairs, there were more people gathered, more wealth, and more commerce than perhaps anywhere else north of the Alps, except in Paris. And certainly much more money changed hands.

The earl's biography tells us that each tournament was announced fifteen days in advance. The news spread. The *esclandre*, the rumor that combat was in preparation at Eu, was thus circulated, it seems, across all of France, Hainaut, Flanders, Burgundy, Poitou, Touraine, Anjou, Normandy, and Brittany in two weeks. Such rapidity over such distances presupposes a perfected communication system, the intervention of a numerous body of informants. The advertising function was performed, we may suppose, by those known as heralds, professionals in identifying and extolling the participants, capable of recognizing all the knights—whose helmets masked their faces—by the heraldic signs they displayed, expert too in the art of composing and interpreting a refrain to launch this team or that champion, lauding their feats and, for a share of the profits, advancing their worth (there was some truth, apparently, in the envious claim that one Henry the Norman was hired to puff William Marshal's reputation). These intermediaries, half poets, half panders, swarmed, it appears, and prospered. The success of the tourneys depended on them. Without resorting to their offices, the promoters could hardly, over a region so vast and a schedule so tight, have circulated a program so dense, so diversified, and enlisting so many participants and supporters.

The announcement chiefly mobilized bachelors, knights without establishment—knights-errant. Still, as I have said, rare were those who arrived alone at the tournament grounds on the morning of the jousts. As a rule, it was in groups that the knights took the field. The large households appeared there in bodies, following their leader or his representative, under a banner flying the colors. Feverish preparations had been made in the public part of the master's residence, in the hall where after dark the household knights stretched out side by side to sleep. The whole of that night had been spent polishing weapons, checking the fit of each piece of armor and harness, furbishing and rolling the chain-mail jerkins and thigh-pieces, mending helms and sword-handles so the joints would be firm, running lacings through the links so the helmet could be attached properly to the shutter and the lining, those protections for the throat and the neck. This was how the basic unit tourneyed: each was the emanation of a house, closely allied by bonds of commensality, recognizable by its rallying cry, as by its patronymic surname and the ensign painted on the shield carried by its members, all comrades accustomed to fight together, to take up where the next man gave out, and to share at the end of the match, under their captain's watchful eye, the profits and glory harvested in the competition. The few isolated figures attempted to join one of these *mesnies* at the last moment; or else reached an agreement among themselves to form one for the occasion, such as those "fifteen knights in company" who had joined together for the Anet tournament, and who on that day called upon William for help when he passed close by their beleaguered troop.

These solidly welded bodies were regrouped upon arrival by the barons organizing the tournament. The great lords had set up camp in advance in their respective lodgings, in the castle or town near the field. They then gathered under their patronage teams that we cannot call national, though each during the engagement conveyed the pride of one ethnic group or another. I believe that the sentiment of belonging to a people, "Franks" or "Angevins," was very strong at the end of the twelfth century, though chiefly negative, as a rejection of the foreigner: I have already pointed out how the English regarded men from Poitou, how the Normans considered being ruled by an Englishman insupportable. And I am convinced that this pride of being from Champagne, from Brittany, or of being French was intensified in these encounters which opposed the team of Champagne against that of Brittany or that of France (by which I mean the ancient duchy of France, center of the Parisian basin). In truth, no more than the national teams of today, those of the twelfth century were not formed of nationals alone. Take the English team led by young Henry and of which William Marshal was both trainer and true captain: for a year and a half this team fought until, by the discretion of its manager, it succeeded, according to our source, in outclassing the others, even the best—the French—who till then, when they saw it appear on the field, had divided up in advance and with laughter "the harness and the sterling" they would soon be stripping it of. While gradually gaining, thanks to William, honor, renown, and the spoils that allowed him to prove himself generous, winning young knights to his team, young Henry engaged all the best horsemen under the English colors; he chose "without bargaining," the text says, "the fine knights of France, Flanders, and Champagne." For the Lagny tournament, he managed to collect an enormous multinational formation: eighty knights, fifteen of them bearing banners—that is leading an already formed team under their ensign—which brought the total forces to two hundred or more. Of this cohort, our text describes the various members in detail and classifies them by the order of their sportive merits. The French are named first, then the Flemish, then the Normans; the English—William Marshal at their head, since he was master of the *hôtel* and his younger brother Anselm among the members—appeared in fourth place on this prize list, followed only by the Angevins.

We may rely on what is minutely reported by the *trouvère* responsible for rhyming William's life: in order to draw up so precise a list, he would certainly refer to the account kept by the clerk in young Henry's service. For if the knights engaged were enumerated so scrupulously, it was because money was involved. In such matters, money counted in those days as much as in ours. And we are distinctly told that these bannerets were in the pay of the English king who daily issued them, from the outset of their residence, twenty *sous* for each horse they brought. Thus Henry owed his success to the ease with which he spent money; his father, not without reason, regarded such prodigality as intolerable: it exceeded that of all the other promoters. A vast commerce thus preceded, accompanied, followed each competition. And the champions put themselves up for auction at the height of their reputations. William Marshal priced his very high in 1183, at the moment when, having roused his lord's rancor, he was fighting on his own: "each lord sought to have him," he declared later on, "and claimed to be willing to pay the high price." These were pensions he was being offered: the count of Flanders and the duke of Burgundy, an income of five hundred *livres*; the advocate of Béthune the same, but solidly based on carefully stipulated lands; Jean d'Avesne, three hundred *livres*, and the lordship of all that was in his power into the bargain. We must not be too credulous of what we may regard as boasting, but the fact remains: the tourney was already a profession in which certain individuals could earn more than anyone else at that time.

The match was fought in broad daylight, in individual combat, like battle itself. Consequently, the various national teams had to regroup into two camps. The distribution was announced in advance. It was known that on a specific day, at a specific time, Angevins, Bretons, and men from Poitou and Le Mans would meet the teams of France, Normandy, and England. South against North this time. But when our text supplies the plan of the joust, certain habitual affinities turn up. Thus Normans and English team up together, and almost always against the French with whom quite naturally the men of Champagne and Burgundy were associated.

T HE GROUND chosen, the "field" (the word is borrowed from the vocabulary of the Judgments of God, that is, of the judiciary duels or from battles, which came down to the same thing, from those formal combats in which two princes agreed to wager all their rights and all their powers), was a vast stretch of countryside, apparently without precise limits, but not without ruggedness. First came what were called the "lists," which seem to be barricades, analogous to the enclosures that in those days fenced in the residences to which the men withdrew to rest, and that custom protected, punishing with heavy penalties those who tried to break into them. The lists, in fact, delimited the "recesses," neutralized regions in which the combatants were entitled, according to the rules of the game, to seek temporary shelter in order to catch their breath, to drink, to recover themselves. In front of these "hedges," before the serious competition began, during the previous evening or well on in the morning, the youngest men, the beginners, paraded, meeting each other in friendly encounters. These were called "litigant jousts": perhaps they differed from the real tournament in the same way that palavers and assemblies of arbitration differed from real combat in wartime. As a matter of fact, these jousts were merely exercises in which, by mutual agreement, overly detrimental blows were avoided. Without danger and without stakes, these combats "for show" were greatly despised by William Marshal; in them there was nothing to win and nothing to lose. In front of the lists were also to be seen, early on the main day, the teams that came to prepare themselves and, still disarmed, to wait for the rest of the company to gather. However, aside from these barricades erected for the requirements of the competition, there existed other obstacles in the open field. Though accidental, they rendered the competition more exciting, for they could be used to set up ambushes or to make an escape. I am speaking of groves, of the rows of vinestocks in a vineyard, of some ancient mound or abandoned earthwork, or else of the "granges," isolated farms whose fields were beginning to be scattered through the countryside in this period. Sometimes it was even a village, whose narrow streets a group of foot soldiers could easily block and which thus became—the inhabitants having obviously cleared out—a kind of minor stronghold in which to wait while the enemy team exhausted itself coursing over the countryside.

On this bristling ground, the tournament opened with certain light figures that the earl's history calls, without describing them, the "commencements." No doubt these were simple processions. The important men did not deign to participate in them: they would bestir themselves later. Meanwhile, they would break their fast, seething with impatience when these opening diversions lasted too long, furious when these youthful matches extended to the point of disturbing the tables where they were taking refreshment. The text does not say whether the real engagement was set off by a signal. When one of the troops considered itself ready, it advanced toward the other: the tournament had begun. The joust consisted, indeed, in hurling oneself upon the adversary. Just as in real battles—the shock of the two mounted troops, the uproar and the thick dust. Two words occur in the very precise, technical vocabulary of the poem, two key words: *férir*, to strike into the mass, and *poindre*, to charge, lance raised, in successive lines, those in the second wave hoping that the first would not have shattered everything, that there would be something left for them to encounter. The goal was to knock down, to pierce, to *outrer* (overthrow), to *défoler* (destroy); to pursue and to overcome those opposite, to disorganize them and finally to provoke their *déconfiture*—their flight in chaos.

At the start, care was taken to preserve formation in both camps, to keep the ranks close, each basic unit, or *conroi*, determined to maintain strict alignment of attack or resistance, so that the front did not give way. This was most difficult of all. In the first place, it was essential that each man master his eagerness to outstrip all the others, the uncontrollable desire to separate oneself from the group in order to "win" more than one's comrades, in honor and profit. The victory, then, fell more often to discipline and self-mastery than to ardor. Once several charges had been made, in the intoxication of blows exchanged, confusion was finally produced in one camp or the other, either from the collison of the small groups too close to each other or too envious of each other, or else from the excess of turbulence, from the uncontrolled explosions of high spirits. The wisest team captains waited for this chaos to occur, holding themselves in reserve until they saw the lines on the opposite side begin to waver and, in places, to break. This was the tactic of the count of Flanders, who did not plunge into the *melee* with his men until the signs of exhaustion and disorder were evident. Then he urged his household "into the breach," with the intention of completely dissociating the already faltering adversary troop, cutting it to pieces, its banners cast down, trampled, divided up into disoriented crews that thought of nothing but flight, pursued, tracked down by the enemy's hordes, taking shelter in each accident of the terrain, at bay and soon surrounded, the day ending in a scattering of stubborn little sieges. This was what *déconfiture* consisted in, and it was considered a marvel when both sides held fast so long that the committee of barons was obliged to institute a truce. By common accord the fighting was stopped, both sides disappointed in the long run, for the strong and the cunning had waited all day long for the chaos of retreat in order to seize more spoils.

For this was the moment when the easiest and most abundant captures could be made. In the tournament, one did not fight only for honor's sake. The knights came here, as to war, to take weapons, harness, and horses and to capture men. To the assured benefits, the wages allotted by the leader of their team, they dreamed of adding their share of booty as well. The great predators were recruited among the bachelors: to the lords, the established figures, such greediness appeared less seemly. In 1198, fifteen years after the Lagny tournament, Richard Coeur de Lion reproached William Marshal for behaving in this fashion—as a young man; he had more than stunned the guardian of the castle of Milly-en-Beauvaisis, splitting his helmet and its lining, and then, somewhat weary, he had simply sat down on the prisoner's body in order that his prey not be stolen from him; this was no longer suitable behavior for his age, nor for his condition as a married man: "to the bachelors, leave the deed, who have yet to pursue their goal." Indeed, in the tournament the barons held back, it appeared, reluctant to take too much for themselves. They tended to focus all their efforts on not being captured. But the others, as soon as they had appeared, even while they were taking their places in the lines, were making their choice among the enemy team and reckoning the value of the trappings they glimpsed at a distance; comparing their own powers with the enemy's, they spied across the field the man they would try to capture at the favorable moment. William Marshal would remember this all his life: the morning of his first tournament he had in one glance—he, a brand-new knight—set his heart upon capturing Messire Philip of Valognes; he had aimed well, since he was able to take this splendid booty, thereby inaugurating a long series of captures. Sometimes, too, certain participants arrived, determined to seize among the throng some victim whom they had failed to take the last time and whom they hated for that reason; the encounter was an occasion to work off one's ill feelings, to satisfy old grudges and new ones as well. In this fashion William hunted down Renaud of Nevers in Maintenon. In any case, the passion was not merely to fight well; certainly the eagerness to take captives or revenge, the custom of selecting in advance, upon sight of the prey, the hostages one meant to keep for oneself, increased the risk of chaos. Especially rare were those combatants who, in all lucidity, set out alone. Generally the hunt for the enemy, like that for game, was conducted in small groups of comrades accustomed to flush out, to pursue, to overcome together. They collaborated to surround, to isolate the man they had "raised." Thus William was beset by five knights at

Saint-Brice, by four at Épernon; at Gournai, seven united adversaries captured the count of Saint-Pol.

B UT IN order to see the sport in all its developments, its feints and faults, is it not best to turn to the text of the *Histoire*, and to one of its episodes? The poem does not describe groups, since the author is following his hero and does not take his eye off him, but precisely, here is our opportunity to be able to place ourselves with him as though at the very heart of the engagement. Hence I am choosing—and not without difficulty, for I should like to be able to take it all —what we are told about one of the tourneys, that at Lagny, and presenting the account virtually as it comes so that the reader can judge the quality of the narrative, or rather—why reject the term?—of the reporting, so that he may delight in the poem's admirable readiness to render life and movement, for all the scarcity of the words and the constraints of the versification. The description begins with the hubbub, in a series of short verses:

> . . . *Grand clangor and great noise.*
> *All were eager to strike home.*
> *Here could you hear the clash*
> *of lance against lance, the pieces*
> *falling so thick upon the ground*
> *the horses could not charge.*
> *Great was the press on the plain.*
> *Each troop shouts its war cry . . .*
> *Here one might see knights taken*
> *and others coming to their rescue.*
> *On all sides were horses to be seen*
> *running and sweating with dread,*
> *Each man eager to do all he could*
> *to win, for in such enterprise*

prowess is quickly seen and shown.
Then would you have seen the earth shake
when the young king said: "Enough,
charge, I shall wait no longer."
The king charged, but the count
[his brother, count of Brittany]
stood fast and wisely did not move . . .
Those then who were about the king
thrust forward with such eagerness
they paid no heed to their king
So far forward did they rush
That they hurled the others back
—it was no retreat but a rout,
when they had forced them to a stand
among the vines, in the ditches.
They went then among the vinestocks
which were thick and heavy on the ground
and there the horses often fell.
Quickly stripped were those who fell
and taken captive, and pitiful . . .
Count Geoffrey with his banner
charged in such strange fashion
when the king came, that all those
who should have been with him were scattered.
Thereupon the king, as he rode up,
could in no place manage to join
with their company, for the enemy fled
and was fiercely pursued the while,
some eager to fight well and nobly,
others eager to win their spoils.
Thus was the king in great alarm
to find himself thus separated.
Upon his right he saw a troop
of enemy soldiers. They might be
forty knights, at the very least.
Holding a lance in his hands

he ran and charged upon them
and so hard struck against them
that his lance broke itself therewith
as if it had been made of glass.
And the enemy abounding there
soon seized him by the rein.
They ran upon him from all sides
whereas it so happened that the king
had none of all his fighting men
but his Marshal who followed him
closely, for he was in the custom
of being at hand, in case of need . . .
And William too, William of Préaux,
who on that day had been captured
and separated from his group,
dressed beneath his tunic
in a coat of mail concealed
and an iron cap upon his head,
and no more nor less than that,
The others were holding in their hands
the king, each of them striving hard
to strike off his helmet . . .
The Marshal then came forward
and flung himself upon them.
So hard he struck, before, behind,
so bravely showed them his mettle
and so drove and so dragged
that he managed to tear away
the headstall of the king's horse
and with it all the harness, pulling.
And William of Préaux took
the horse by the neck and made
great efforts to emerge from the battle,
for many were fighting around him
who sought to hold him back.
He struggled mightily, to strike,

and often, that William of Préaux.
The king astutely covered him
with his shield, that he be not hurt
nor that any man do him harm.
But others in the fight strove
so hard they tore away the king's
helmet and sore offended him.
The struggle lasted a long time
and was joined mightily the while
by the Marshal, who fought hard
and heavily, distributing great blows . . .
While the king was in this pass,
Messire Herloin of Vancy
—seneschal of the count of Flanders—
had some thirty horses
kept from the press of battle.
One of his knights ran up
and came to speak with the Lord Herloin.
"In God's name," quoth he, "sweet lord,
see there, the king about to be taken.
Come, take him. Yours will be the prize.
He has already lost his helmet
and stands amazed in great confusion."
When Messire Herloin heard him
he delighted greatly at the words
and said: "I believe he is ours."
All spurred on their steeds
with great address, after the king.
The Marshal did not wait one moment
but charged, his lance fixed, at them.
He struck them so dreadfully
that his lance splintered altogether.

(Here a verse or two are missing from the manuscript, doubtless describing William Marshal thrown back by the shock
and nearly unhorsed.)

> *. . . to the hock of his horse.*
> *But all was perfectly recovered.*
> *Upon him, as in a battle,*
> *they flung themselves to the assault*
> *and he defended himself against them,*
> *all that he strikes, he strikes down,*
> *cracks shields, splits helmets.*
> *So mightily did William Marshal fight*
> *that none of those who were there*
> *knew what had become of the king.*
> *Later on, the king was to say,*
> *and all those who had seen him,*
> *and those who heard speak of him,*
> *that never was such a feat seen*
> *or heard of from a single knight,*
> *finer than the Marshal's on that day.*
> *The best men praised him mightily.*

Such praises are excessive, of course. Like the romance or the *chanson de geste*, the panegyric improperly isolates its hero from the group besetting him and accentuates the singular exploit. But it shows with wonderful explicitness that the tourney consists first of all in taking prisoners, as well as the ways of doing so. The most expeditious and also the most praiseworthy method is to "knock down" the opposing knight, to unhorse him with a single thrust of the lance.

We learn from other passages in the biography that the victorious jouster frequently stopped there, hesitating to try double or nothing; he would leave the unhorsed knight flat on the ground and walk away, leading his horse with him. At the Eu tournament, William Marshal thus twice threw Matthew of Walincourt, both times seizing his charger—the same one. To unseat the opposing knight passed among connoisseurs for the most successful figure of this entire military ballet. And loudest of all was the applause for those who took the high barons for their targets. As in real battles, the

ultimate goal was—we have just seen Herloin of Vancy lick-
ing his chops over it in advance—to unhorse the leaders or
to capture them. When a count of Clermont fell, then got up
again and remounted his horse like Philip Augustus at Bouvines, the feat was talked of "far and long." In truth, such
successes were rare. First of all because only the most valorous and the boldest ventured into battle in this fashion. The
cowardly were much more chary of themselves, keeping
their distance from overly brutal skirmishes. Consequently,
no one felt dishonored by falling; the poem puts it nicely: "it
is under the horses' hooves that the champions are to be
sought."

Further, we learn that the lances were fragile and generally
splintered before the adversary fell beneath the charge.
Those warriors who risked themselves in the fray knew how
to stay in the saddle and to control their mount. They did not
avoid the impact, but held fast. Then the struggle continued
hand to hand, with sword and club. Blows were aimed at the
helmet. For this reason, head armor was considerably developed at the time. The simple iron cap did not seem adequate protection; it was abandoned to the squires and foot
soldiers. The helmet was tending, at the end of the twelfth
century, to assume the shape (it had done so forty years later,
when the biographer was writing) of a closed box, and closed
so hermetically that the combatant risked asphyxiation if he
came too near a brush fire. (William had a taste of this expe-
rience one day, to his cost.) In order to overcome one's adversary, to capture him, it was therefore necessary either to
strip him of this piece of armor to lay his head bare—and if
young Henry was so "offended" to be thus denuded, it was
doubtless not only for having lost his main defense; there
was also an element of shame involved—or else to stun him
by striking with all one's might against what covered the
skull. William Marshal remembered having been thus im-
prisoned by his own helmet several times, blinded and rendered incapable of ridding himself of it, either because the

helmet had turned round back to front under the impact, or else because it had been so wrenched out of shape that it was necessary, at the tournament's end, to resort to the blacksmith's services—to lay one's head on the anvil until it could be extracted by hammer and tongs from the iron envelope, finally decorticated after great exertion.

When, still mounted, one's chosen prey was so dazed, deafened, and weakened that he no longer saw clearly or knew where to strike, the moment had come to take his horse "by the rein," to lead it out of the *melee*, toward the armsyard in care of the squires and seconds. To leave the field in this way with one's living booty would disturb the combat group, and the captains' most difficult task, in tournaments as in real battles, consisted in delaying enterprises of capture until the enemy's disarray had turned into a rout, when the other side was entirely demoralized, when the most tempting victims—as was the case when Messire Herloin decided to intervene—were no longer protected by their servants. But to lead one's prisoner to a safe place was not always easy, for the stunned man's friends would rush to his rescue. As did William, who kept watch over the king, his ward and pupil. Sometimes the captive, recovering after a while from the daze inflicted by helmet blows, would give rein to his horse and escape; or else the horse would release itself by rearing; sometimes, too, the rider would abandon his mount and manage to escape, like Messire Simon of Neauphle, who grabbed in passing a low gutter in the village street where William Marshal had captured him; turning round, William no longer saw anything but the horse: whereupon much laughter on either side. For this extremely brutal sport, as we note at each line of the story, was also an extremely gleeful one. Hence it was prudent, when one had the strength to do so, immediately to secure the captive whose value was greater than that of his horse, to seize him bodily, and having pitched him over the saddlebow, to carry him off alive. William boasted of having performed this feat several times.

When he had finally been carried to a safe place, the captured knight set foot on the ground, acknowledged himself a prisoner, and gave his word; his captor entrusted the horse to his own men. As for the vanquished knight, henceforth confined to the sidelines he watched the end of the combat as a spectator, judging the blows, advising the participants who were his friends. Sometimes, like William of Préaux, he gave a helping hand. Cheating a bit. What was one's word, at such moments, compared to the desire, indeed the passion, to "strike" and to "charge"? Unless the oral promise authorized the defeated knights in certain circumstances to plunge back into the thick of things. How else explain that certain knights admitted to having been captured several times in the same day?

When one side was scattered in defeat, or else when at nightfall it was decided—everyone being exhausted—to stop and to attribute the victory on points, the combatants did not immediately separate. On the field and its margins, the throng remained quite as dense, but for peaceful transactions. It no longer had the appearance of a battle, it assumed that of a fair. No more blows or battle cries, nor was the uproar now so much the clatter of arms as the clink of money being counted out. In the first place, it was essential to dress wounds and to strip off the warped and dented armor—which was not always an easy matter. Then each man inquired after friends lost to sight in the complications of the skirmish: were they captive, wounded, dead? The leading knights, helmets off, abandoned themselves to the pleasure of showing off, palavering among themselves in the presence of the young, discussing the match. After having competed for valor, they were competing for courtesy and wisdom by exchange of words, not blows, in interminable speeches, all night long. There was a continual coming and going from tent to tent. The combat was criticized. An attempt was made, by juxtaposing partial reports, to reconstruct in its entirety the progress of the tourney, to distribute prizes and praises fairly. Thus an honors list was gradually established, and the combatants, at the end of each encounter, were reclassified as a result of their day's exploits. It was incumbent on the heralds and the *minstrels* to make the classification public. On it depended the amount of the wages the participants would demand next time from the team leaders.

Nonetheless by nightfall, in shadows that were not always safe (at Épernon William's charger was stolen from him at the very door of the house where he had gone to greet Count Thibaut), the force of the discussion turned on the spoils. In actual warfare, at the skirmish's end, the leaders of the groups habitually "divided up the booty," entirely turned over to them: thus at Milly William led the horse he had taken to the captain of his team: it was then King Richard who, out of generosity, left it to him. What happened in the tournaments? It seems as if the same rules were followed: When Matthew of Walincourt sought to obtain free restitution of the horse William had seized during combat, he did not claim it from his vanquisher but from the latter's lord, young Henry. In any case, countless transactions were conducted on the evening after each competition: estimating, counting, repaying. "Promised" men were worrying about the friends who would set them free, paying the ransom that had been agreed upon; if they failed to do so, which was common enough, they would set out in search of either guarantees or hostages to put into their "master's" hands. Those of humbler nature begged for release, or for the return of gear they had been stripped of, asking that at least half of it be restored to them. The victors, including William Marshal of course, at the end of each tournament entertained themselves, using the money that now flowed so freely between their fingers and that they did not know what to do with, as the good knights they claimed to be. It was an astonishment, in fact, for those who were generally short of coins to be so rich. Thus one saw an impecunious knight indulging himself in the luxury of paying ready money for what he was buying, laying out in a single gesture five thousand five hundred pieces of silver, or else casually dicing away his winnings. And if he won—William Marshal of course always won—abandoning himself to the eminent pleasure of giving presents to everyone, to the less fortunate, to those who had been taken prisoner that day, emptying his purse and leaving his own prisoners marveling at all they still owed him. It was perhaps only that—this extravagant and necessary liberality —which distinguished the tournament from war in which captives, even those of noble blood, were much more severely treated, like those whom the leader of the Marcade mercenaries dragged in chains behind him with nooses round their necks, as if they were hounds on the leash. The tournament was a festivity. It ended like all festivities in the careless scattering of wealth; and the knights, victors and vanquished alike, all went to sleep poorer than they had wakened. Only the merchants—the parasites—had profited.

C ONSEQUENTLY the earl, victorious, if we are to believe him, in every tournament—at least once he had managed, after a year and a half of fumbling exercises, to raise the English team to the first rank—did not enrich himself during this period of his life. He confessed as much to the mercenary Sancho, quite sincerely and not to obtain mercy: "I, a poor bachelor, who owns not one furrow of land." Yet in seven years he had captured hundreds of knights. Five hundred at least, he said on his deathbed. At the Eu tournament alone, he took ten in a single day, and twelve horses, with saddles and "gear," one of them twice over. In order to profit by the profession and because it was better to use both hands than one, he had accepted the offer of a knight from the same *mesnie*, Roger of Gaugi, a Fleming "doughty in arms, valiant and bold." Roger suggested that the two of them form a society, as the merchants were doing, to share profits and losses. Thus the pair constituted, within young

111

Henry's close-knit *hôtel*, an even more interdependent labor group. This "company" lasted two years, and together they earned much more than others grouped together in sixes and eights. The author of the *Histoire* cites his proofs, the accounts kept by the servants in charge of records, and notably Wigain, the young king's kitchen clerk—and this confirms in passing that all the prizes went to the leaders of the bands. Between Pentecost and the following Lent, William and Roger together captured a hundred and three knights; as for chargers and gear, the scribes did not bother to list them. All the same, in a magnificent gesture, tossing on the tables the sacks of coin just acquired for their mutual entertainment, renouncing with a smile all pressure on his prisoners, fighting for the mere pleasure of winning, William Marshal kept nothing for himself, except glory.

By 1178, he had gained complete supremacy over the heir of Henry II, and had made his way to the highest level of aristocratic society. The leading nobles treated him as an equal. Now he was listened to in the evening conversations. After 1179, the earl of Huntingdon and Cambridge deferred to him; he had precedence over other bannerets, and no longer conducted himself modestly but strutted about everywhere, making a great show of his pride. He may have committed certain indiscretions, playing without sufficient skill the difficult game of courtly love with the queen. The fact is that William became intolerable in the *hôtel*. His comrades, as we know, laid a trap for him, their calumny or spite destroying the loving link that attached William to their common lord and thereby ruining him. He kept only one friend, Baldwin, the young son of the advocate of Béthune. At the beginning of 1183, just forty years old, denied the court and the royal table, he was reduced to behaving like a very young man, like a knight-errant, because he had no savings. All he owned he carried on his back. This was something, in truth, for he was most attached to the luster of his equipage, most concerned to make a great show of elegance and to eclipse all rivals, exhibiting the most brilliant weapons of the very latest model. In order to care for all this gear and, like the barons, show himself in fine fettle, he took a squire into his service; at the Lagny fair, he paid out thirty *livres* for a second charger that, he recalled—adding to the glory of having been able to spend so much that of knowing more about horseflesh than the trader—was worth at least fifty.

This splendid gear matched his reputation, which was so certain that he might have immediately hired himself out, and at a high price, to some other master. He was greatly sought after, in fact. The count of Flanders, the duke of Burgundy had ridden after him high and low, and now offered him golden bridges to their service: he refused all but temporary engagements; doubtless it was to one of these that he owed the acquisition of the little Flemish fief we know he possessed. He might also, if we are to believe what memory has retained, have been able to settle down, leaving his bachelor youth behind—might have taken a wife and founded his own household: the advocate of Béthune apparently offered him his own daughter, as well as an income of a thousand *livres*. William affected to be not yet *en courage* to marry—he had no such intention, but offered thanks. It satisfied his pride to have seen a count of Saint-Pol approaching him at a gallop as he was making his way in January 1183, over the Gournai tournament grounds, greeting him, kissing him, urging him to join the others he was leading to combat—and he, William Marshal, declining such an honor of course, feigning to stand on a lower level, to respect the hierarchy of titles and ranks, but accepting such company as an equal: the count had no good horses left, and William lent him one of his own two chargers. How he savored the pleasure of publicly establishing his brotherhood with this very noble baron, who numbered thirty knights beneath his banner—as a big brother, of course, since William greatly outstripped him in prowess throughout this most successful tournament!

At its end, we can consider him at the zenith of his jousting fame. He then has the coquetry to vanish almost immediately, escaping those who sought to secure him at all costs, on the pretext of a pilgrimage to Cologne, to visit the relics of the Three Wise Men. A gesture of symbolic piety, since in William's mind, if not his biographer's, the three kings had suffered Herod's unjustified suspicion, as he himself had been victimized by his young lord's. And William proclaims his hope of obtaining, by this holy journey, a miracle: to be washed clean of the suspicion of adultery that weighs upon him. Thereby he makes an appeal—to heaven. But more directly to his former lord, whose love he is inconsolable at having lost. So doing, William has his wits about him. He knows perfectly well that he will never derive a greater profit from his valor than by regaining the affection of England's young king. To this end, he makes certain that the royal entourage hears of his recent exploits; it is clear that he has no need of the herald Henry the Norman's services nor of further victories in order to recruit companions; propositions he has rejected. He is waiting to be recalled, trusting to the discretion of Baldwin of Béthune. He does not have to wait long. Indeed, once Lent is over, young Henry breaks with his father, wages war against him once more, and comes in search of allies.

The young king summons a very limited council one evening—only three knights are present: his brother Geoffrey, count of Brittany, the sire de Lusignan, and Roger of Gaugi, lately an associate of William Marshal and obviously his partisan. But Geoffrey too takes up his defense, eager for him to return to favor: Henry, he says, can find no better counselor in combat. As for the sire de Lusignan, though despised by William, who regards him as the instigator of Patrick of Salisbury's murder, he offers to fight in single combat in order to defend the queen and William Marshal, maintaining that the accusations brought against them are without basis. Young Henry is convinced. He dismisses the leader of the opposition party, that traitor who had taken his victim's place at the head of the *mesnie*. William is sent for. The household chamberlain sets out, scours the highways in vain, returns empty-handed, exhausted. By chance, he falls in with William, who is returning from Cologne fresh and in fine fettle and who learns, with many thanks to heaven, that his prayers have been answered. Such is the virtue of pilgrimages. Pious, William is also wary. He seeks assurance that adultery will never be mentioned again; that once he has returned, he will not be taken at his word and invited, as once offered, to engage in trial by combat, one finger cut off, or against three successive champions. Moreover, to accept means to be caught up in the dispute between father and son. William is determined not to incur the old king's wrath, to burn no bridges, and to take no sides; he rejoins young Henry's camp only with old Henry's consent.

Here we see more clearly than ever the nature of war in those times: it was merely one of the explicit aspects of an interminable discord. Warfare itself never went on for long. Ceaselessly interrupted by embraces, by simulacra of reconciliation, by truces, it was always waged on the surface and unlikely to damage the network of relations that formed the armature of knightly society. Adversaries fought, sometimes perhaps more brutally than on the tournament grounds when hatreds grew intense, but without this more violent sport reaching the point of seriously jeopardizing the bonds of blood, of vassalage, of knighthood, and of companionship. It required accidents, an ill-measured blow, killing by mistake, for the links to be broken, for rancor to feed the spirit of revenge. Yet here too, each man had to respect the rules, to speak and to listen before passing from one side to the other. In the chamberlain's name, the young king therefore agreed to a postponement. William Marshal rode to the court of France, where he counted many friends; let it be known that he was henceforth exonerated and that no one would further inquire into his relations with the sister of Philip Augustus; asked for and obtained letters from the king, from his uncle the archbishop of Rheims, from his cousin Robert of Dreux, from Count Theobald of Blois, the providence of all who fought in tournaments. These letters-patent were sent to the old English king, soliciting him to authorize the libeled man to resume his functions. Henry II could not do otherwise than to send William Marshal his own letters-patent. By refusing, he would have let it be supposed that he continued to give credence to the rumors. He permitted William to rejoin his lord and thereby gave him leave to wage war against himself, but assured him that the love he bore him would not thereby be diminished.

No sooner had William Marshal, escorted by his friend Baldwin and by Hugh de Hamelincourt, returned to the fold than the young king died of a sudden disease on June 11, 1183. This was a bitter blow. The *mesnies* fell apart as soon as their leader perished; by a sudden turn of the wheel of fortune, those at the summit found themselves reduced to begging their bread from door to door. All of William's hopes collapsed. His lord, contrary to all expectations had perished before his father, and in the very course of the war he was waging against that father—a war William was waging as well. An authorized war. But how sincere was the love promised by the letters-patent? How would Henry II regard him now? He would of course pardon his late son, but that son's servants? More anxious than any of these, William led the knights of the *hôtel:* their duty was to bear their lord's embalmed corpse from Quercy, where he had died, to his father first of all, then to Notre-Dame de Rouen, where young Henry had chosen to await resurrection among his ancestors, the Norman dukes. Another worry—minor but obsessive: the treasury, as usual, was empty and creditors were blocking the road; it was at this point that William Marshal was obliged to guarantee himself for a hundred silver *marcs* to Sancho the mercenary. Henry II did not flinch when William described his son's unknown disease, his sufferings, his last sigh, and his contrition. Without argument he paid all his wastrel son's debts. In his grief, he did not cavil and caused the hundred *marcs* to be issued; he released William, but went no further. With Baldwin and Hugh, William Marshal was obliged to resume fighting in tournaments.

Fortunately he was a crusader. Young Henry, like so many knights at this time, had vowed to set off as soon as possible on a pilgrimage to Jerusalem. On his deathbed, in the great scene of his final agony, when he was dictating his testament, he had bequeathed his cross to William, master of the household, his natural substitute, instructing him to "carry it to the Holy Sepulcher and pay his debt to God." This gift was received in great honor. The mission was not a disagreeable one. Aside from the benefits it would afford the soul and the pleasures expected from an excursion to faraway parts, it would offer the occasion, in these difficult times, to cover ground, to let time pass, and to see what was coming. And under the most favorable conditions: according to custom, crusaders preparing to take the holy journey were loaded with gifts of money, horses, and gear of all kind, for they appeared as proxies of all those who for the moment hesitated to take such a long journey. In the days of his prosperity, William Marshal had been very generous to crusaders. Now he made a preliminary excursion to England where custom obliged him, on such an occasion, to say farewell to his "friends in the flesh"; he visited his sisters, women whom he had not seen for so many years, to whom he was attached by memories of earliest childhood, and who now represented his entire line, since he had no heir. Upon leaving, he bequeathed them what little he owned. Indeed, a man leaving for the Holy Land stripped himself as for the approach of death. Was it not the crusaders' hope to win in that country the finest, the surest mortality, guarantee of all indulgences? Did they not dream of being buried, at the term of that peregrination, alongside the saints in the Valley of Jehosephat, thereby occupying the first ranks among the resurrected cohorts? William, too, may well have expected such a reward. But he now had good reasons to hope, if he survived, if he returned, to resume his place at the heart of a royal household—that ot the old king. When he had made his visit to Henry Plantagenet, seeking authorization to leave, the king had urged him not to delay: he had need of him. While he gave him one hundred *livres* in Anjou *deniers* as traveling money, he took from him two of the horses William had received from other donors. They would be, he said, the pledge of his prompt return.

THE BIOGRAPHER has preserved nothing of the memories of this crusade. Such an omission surprises us. John d'Erley, of course, the chief informant, was not yet in William's service. But did not William describe his own exploits overseas, as he had described his tournaments? Had he remained silent about this splendid adventure? Perhaps. He may have respected that precept of the Templars' order, of which he returned a member, forbidding any vain boastfulness. Unless we assume that our copy of the original manuscript is incomplete. All it tells us, in any case, is that William spent two years in Syria, that he performed as much there by way of high deeds and *largesse* as others in seven, and that he served King Guy of Jerusalem and won the love of the Templars, of the Hospitalers, of all . . . We find him returning in 1187, a few months before news reached the West that the True Cross was once again in infidel hands, like Jerusalem soon afterward.

William Marshal had hurried back to Henry II, who "retained" him, as he had promised, among the knights of his *hôtel*. The old monarch was failing, beginning to lose his footing. He trusted the English to withstand the rebellions that were troubling his Continental domains. William established himself among the king's "familiars." This position was not without its dangers: the master, it was obvious, did not have long to live. His son Richard, impatient to succeed, opposed him furiously. Everything suggested that he would treat his father's friends harshly. In truth, William Marshal had no choice. He himself was beginning to show the signs of age. Scarcely a dozen years younger than Henry II, he was approaching the age when the stiffening knights prepared to die. In any case, there could be no question of resuming the life of tournaments, of once again enjoying those pleasures, of harvesting those ready profits: in the emotion that followed the debacle of the Latin states of the Holy Land, knighthood lent a more obedient ear to the Church's injunctions; military sports were suspended as a measure of penitence while a new general expedition was being prepared. Wars, of course, continued. William led them to the best of his ability, as only he knew how to do, in the service of his new lord. For him he put his own body in danger, confronting the warriors of the king of France at Montmirail, between Châteaudun and Le Mans, and in other skirmishes, defending the moribund king against his sons' endless aggressions, which Philip Augustus, openly or not, provoked and supported.

Meanwhile, William Marshal felt in his limbs the onset of age and knew that soon he would no longer be of much use in arms, that he would no longer be paid wages, that he must join, in the tedium of a Temple commandery, some peevish group of valetudinarian warriors. It seemed a matter of some urgency to obtain, while there was still time—while Henry II survived—a solid reward, one that would assure him a position and stable resources for the imminent moment when his profession would become too painful and no longer afford him a livelihood. He remained a poor man. Upon his return from the crusades, his master had indeed granted him a fief in England, the lands of Cartmel in Lancashire, but this was very modest; thirty-two *livres* annual revenue—the price of the horse he had bought, not so long ago, at the Lagny fair. His poverty, as he had so accurately told Sancho, was a consequence of the fact that he was still a bachelor. Hence what he wanted, at nearly fifty, was to cease to be so, to receive at last a wife who might be a rich heiress, to establish her at once in his bed, in his house, in his seigneury. If he had four years ago rejected the daughter offered him by Robert de Béthune, this was perhaps because she brought to the marriage only income and not the land and seigneurial powers of which he dreamed. It is more likely, as I have said, that he was keeping himself in reserve. He wanted to be married by the king of England—one of the two—by the young man he served, if not by his father. For it was notorious that the king of England could draw upon a copious reservoir of husbandless women, many of whom were worth a great deal. Custom constantly fed this reservoir, authorizing the sovereign to marry off the widows and orphans of his deceased vassals, to distribute them judiciously among the bachelors attached to him, as the wages of their good service. Indeed, this was how he ruled, how he controlled more closely than by any other artifice, the nobles of his realm and the lesser men as well. No one could ask for a more profitable gift: this one immediately effected a change of condition, a transformation from the total dependence of younger sons to the security of the *seniores*.

The king consented, gave William his seneschal's daughter (the father having died three years before without male heir), the "damsel of Lancaster," and, to enjoy after the wedding, her *tènement*, the fief her father had held from the crown. This woman was not yet nubile. While he waited for her to become so, she was entrusted to her future husband, who "held her in great honor and protected her from dishonor [which means that he resisted immediately taking his pleasure of the child, as many in his condition would have done] a long while, as his dear friend." "Friend," but not wife. For two years later, in May 1189, judging himself increasingly indispensable in the harsh fighting that had resumed in Maine, he asked for more and received it. In order to satisfy him, Henry II, whose sickness was growing worse, the swellings in his groin becoming boils, picked up his cards, shuffled and redealt them. Gilbert Fitzrenfrew, his new seneschal, obtained the "damsel of Lancaster," discarding, in order to take her, the heiress he had in hand, who passed to Renaud Fitzherbert. Baldwin of Béthune now took the heiress of Châteauroux, while his old friend William Marshal found himself granted the morsel he coveted, the "damsel of Striguil." Here he drew a winning card: Helvis of Lancaster meant only one knight's fief; Isabel of Striguil, sixty-five-and-a-half fiefs: here we can measure the preponderance William Marshal had assumed in two years over the king, who was dying so rapidly, in truth, that he would have to make haste to seize what was falling from his royal hands. Unfortunately, William could not wed then and there. The succulent heiress had been living in the Tower of London during the thirteen years since her father's death, kept there out of harm's way. This was a treasure so precious that the king could not bring himself to part with her. Hubert Gauthier, then clerk of the grand justiciar of England, finally received orders that the girl and the land be swiftly delivered. Henry II died even more swiftly, on July 6, 1189.

A second blow, much harsher than the first, for William had inspired the hatred of Richard Coeur de Lion, the new king, only a month before. The old sovereign, pursued by his son and the French knights, had withdrawn from the burning city of Le Mans. Intoxicated by his victory, Richard, then count of Poitiers, had leaped on his horse without taking the time to buckle on his armor. He wore no helmet, merely an iron cap, no shirt of mail, merely a leather jerkin. William Marshal's duty was to cover the retreat, as his father had once covered Matilda's, as he himself, at Lagny, had protected young Henry against the assault of those preparing to capture him. He rode to meet the aggressor with his sword and his pike. Dialogue:

> *By God's legs, Marshal,*
> *kill me not, that would be wrong*
> *for I am all unarmed."*
> *And William Marshal answered:*
> *"No. Let the Devil kill you*
> *for I shall not . . . "*

It would have been easy enough to do: Richard was not sheathed in metal. William spared him, but struck the horse with his lance and killed the animal. The count fell. "This was a fine stroke," and one that saved from capture, or worse, those who fled in disarray.

To kill the heir-apparent's horse under him in a tournament—*a fortiori* in the more severe engagements of actual warfare—was not without consequences, nor was sending him to be killed by the Devil. Such formulas were taken literally in the period, and such words possessed a terrible power. Hence, while William was leading old Henry's funeral procession toward Fontevrauld, everyone wondered. Soon the new king would appear at the funeral: "The count will come; we have been for his father, against him; he will be wroth at heart against us for it." To which the worldly-wise replied; "The world is not all in his hands. We may escape his mastery, and if we find it meet to change lords, God will grant us His grace. For ourselves, we fear nothing, but we fear for William Marshal. Yet he must know of it; so long as we have horses, arms, money and gear, he shall have what he needs." And William replied; "It is true that I have killed the horse, nor do I repent of it. For your offers, I give you thanks, but it would shame me to take your gifts, if I could not restore them to you. God nonetheless showed me His great goodness when I was a knight; and to Him I trust myself and my hopes." Trust and faith. In his heart of hearts, in truth, William Marshal was anxious indeed. It was known that Richard was impulsive and rancorous. Doubtless a death sentence seemed unlikely at the time of his joyous accession, but if William managed to save his skin, what chance did he now have of plucking the fruit of his long service, the splendid gift the late king had made him, his golden dream? The "damsel of Striguil"—how would he manage to obtain her?

Enter Richard, impassive. Upon his appearance, no one can detect either anger or pleasure, nor even uneasiness. He stops in front of the body, leans over it, and remains pensive for a long moment. Then of all those who had sided with his father, he summons only William Marshal and Messire Maurice de Craon, as well as his own friends: "Let us leave this place." Outside, a little group forms around the prince: his first royal council. He speaks, and his first words are to say, "Marshal, the other day, you sought to kill me, and dead I should surely be if I had not turned your lance aside with my arm. That would have been an evil day for you." "Sire, I had no intention of killing you, nor did I ever try to do so. I am still strong enough to direct my lance. If I had wished, I should have struck your body, as I did your horse. If I killed the horse, I did not do so by mistake, nor do I repent doing so." "Marshal, I pardon you. Never shall I bear you rancor for it." First—and crucial—relief. William will not suffer corporal punishment. There remains the "damsel of Striguil." Immediately the question is raised, but by someone else: "Sire, do not take it badly. I would remind you that the king your father gave her to Marshal." "By God's legs, he did not. He but promised to do so. But I will give her to him freely, both the lady and the lands." Which is to say, the essentials. Richard is thanked by all. William Marshal dare not believe his luck—he has had a narrow escape.

Whereupon he is seen riding at breakneck speed to take possession, to wed. He is instructed, with Gilbert Pipart, to go to England to guard Richard's lands and his rights. In two days, they cross Anjou, Maine, and Normandy, leap into a boat at Dieppe; the deck collapses beneath their weight. Pipart, with a broken arm, remains on the bank; William, also wounded in the leg, clings to the rigging, then makes his way across England, greets on his way through Winchester old Queen Eleanor, who has been liberated by her widowhood and is radiant. He reaches London. The grand justiciar, the damsel's guardian, first presents a deaf ear, bargains, and finally relinquishes her in self-defense. William insists upon carrying her off immediately. He burns to consummate the marriage, but he wants the wedding to take place upon her own lands. For this is important. By wedding an heiress, the young groom establishes himself as lord and master, but of an alien patrimony, that of his wife's ancestors; he knows that the uncles and cousins are rebellious, and the former master's entire *mesnie* jealous of seeing a man of another blood ruling there because he possesses this woman. Hence it is prudent to solemnize the festivity, the public ceremonial of the nuptials, in that very house. As an affirmation of his rights. Besides, William is "a poor bachelor"—where, if not in the wife's realm, would he find the wherewithal to pay for the largesse, the ample expenditures of generosity necessary for any nuptial solemnity? All the same, the host who has lodged him in London urges him to remain, makes him comfortable: he will pay everything. William yields, consents to copulate on the spot. Yet he must have a bed. Sire Engerrand de Abernon lends him one, at some distance—at Stokes. Isabel is in his arms. He is nearly fifty. At last he has left his youth behind. On this night, applying himself to deflowering the damsel of Striguil, to getting her with child, he has crossed the line, has gone over to the right side, the side of the seigneurs. His fortune—nothing more is needed—his very great fortune is made.

5

RICHARD Fitzgilbert de Clare, Isabel's father, had taken a legitimate wife in 1171 and died in 1176. In those days when custom decreed a daughter must be twelve before she could be put in a husband's bed, Isabel was certainly of age, but she was at most seventeen, about thirty years younger than her husband, a man on the wane. Chances were considerable that this woman would soon be a widow, and a very desirable one, returning to the hands of the appointed matchmaker, the king, to serve a second time as a sumptuous reward for valorous services. Who could foresee, on her wedding day, that she would live some thirty years more in the shadow of William Marshal's astonishing longevity? That he would enjoy her body so long and so arduously that she would give him at least ten children? That he would exploit for so many years the rights his marriage had entitled him to administer? These rights were enormous: only one other heiress in all England was richer than Isabel at the time.

Since 1096 the Clares had possessed the castle of Striguil on the Severn, opposite Bristol; they also held Goodrich fortress nearby. The head of this house was the earl of Pembroke, one of that group of barons who governed the Welsh marches, responsible for containing the ceaseless rebellions from that direction and empowered, the better to accomplish this difficult task, with exceptional privileges. The king of England, though jealous of all royal prerogatives, had granted them to these frontier barons. The earl of Pembroke, like the other "palatine" barons, possessed powers over these marches comparable to those of the great feudatories of the king of France. Through her father, Isabel also claimed the inheritance of a great Norman line that had died out in 1164: her great-great-grandfather, at the end of the eleventh century, had married a Giffard. She could not obtain the whole inheritance, obliged to share it with a cousin, the earl of Hertford, but the castle of Orbec, near Lisieux, had come to her, and half the barony of Longueville: two manors and the service of forty-three knights. A splendid seigneury, as we can reckon from the inheritance tax, two thousand silver *marcs*, which the king demanded of William before authorizing him to "collect," as the expression went, this fief and to hold it in his wife's name. And finally, through her mother, Isabel possessed nearly a fourth of Ireland. In 1170, sailing in fact from Pembroke, Henry Plantagenet had undertaken to conquer that island. He had sent announcements to Rome that this country was plunged into intolerable disorder, causing the Church great suffering. By the gold ring with which he invested him, the pope had charged the king to wage war there, virtually a crusade. A difficult task, but one made easier by the harsh and constant disputes among the clans and their minor chiefs, who called themselves kings. One of these, Dermot, king of Leinster, in order to prevail over his rivals, allied himself with the invader and gave his daughter to one of the English leaders, Richard de Clare, nicknamed "Richard Strongbow." The latter brutally pacified the kingdom, drove out the troublemakers, and soon was master of the region; Henry II kept for himself the ports of Dublin, Wexford, and Waterford, but Richard received as a fief the entire interior around the stronghold of Kilkenny. The land was poor, the natives recalcitrant, almost as dangerous as the Welsh; hence strong forces were required to control them, and it was necessary that the new king of Ireland—in 1177, Henry II had raised his son John Lackland to this dignity— grant the sire of Leinster prerogatives as sweeping as those the earl of Pembroke possessed in England. The Irish inheritance certainly constituted the most brilliant part of William Marshal's match: his wife was a king's granddaughter, and she prided herself upon the fact. The *Song of Dermot*, which describes the conquest of Leinster and celebrates her father and grandfather, appears to have been commissioned by Isabel, as her husband's history was subsequently commissioned by her son in the same spirit of family pride. Let us add that Leinster brought in great revenues—seventeen thousand *livres* a year in the middle of the thirteenth century, at the death of Isabel's youngest son: five hundred times more than Cartmel; in concrete terms, the value of about four hundred pure-bred chargers.

In truth, though he had agreed to give Isabel (with her *ténement*) in marriage, Richard Coeur de Lion kept a good share of the inheritance for himself. We see how advantageous the sovereign's power to marry off daughters and widows of the great vassals could be: keeping these women as his wards, the king appropriated for the crown, apart from what the guardian to whom he entrusted them kept for himself, the profits of their patrimony. When he finally handed them over to one or another of his friends, he drove a hard bargain for the privilege, and in particular delayed granting the seigneurial rights that might limit his own sovereignty. The gift seemed of such value to the groom, hitherto a nobody, that he consented to such encroachments without too much objection, saying nothing for the moment, biding his time, thanking the king but hoping too that eventually— supported by comrades who would come to testify to the custom, to swear that as far back as they could remember his predecessors had done this or that—he could take possession of the whole cake. A secret little struggle developed between the parvenus-by-marriage and the crown, which was stubbornly seeking to recover some of the royal prerogatives that necessities of defense had previously forced the king to grant to the border nobles. Therefore William was to wait more than ten years before receiving the earl's sword for

Pembroke; in Leinster, he never managed to gain all the rights of his office.

In 1189, after the wedding, he nonetheless was exultant. We see him immediately showing his gratitude to Providence for such magnificent favor, for having made him so immediately rich. On the only land that was his own, Cartmel, he founds an ecclesiastical establishment that will offer perpetual thanks to heaven in his name; in this priory he installs regular canons whom he takes—we may note this—from Bradenstoke, the lineal sanctuary of his mother's ancestors where his older brother will soon choose to be buried. No sooner is William in possession of a wife than he is concerned —modestly still, for his sudden fortune intimidates him—to establish a place of prayers for his descendants, cheerfully sacrificing for this purpose the little wealth he has already won by his own powers. He has no hesitation in doing so: through his wife he is henceforth a thousand times better provided for.

Over his wife he keeps watch as over the most precious treasure in the world. It appears that she accompanies him wherever he goes. When the king, his lord, orders him to Normandy, he takes Isabel with him. All the power he claims to possess—at Longueville and in other places—emanates from the person, from the "head" of Isabel; it is indispensable that his wife be seen there at his side, that every eye recognize her as his, acknowledging that he shares her bed, that they make one flesh, that consequently homage must be paid to this husband, who must form his own court and safeguard his honor in every fashion. Such a necessity obliges him to embark in his own ship when he sails to Ireland in 1207 for the first time. And when he is almost immediately recalled by John Lackland, who eventually comes to hate him and whose maneuvers he fears—the men of his council are similarly suspicious, convinced that the king summons him "by design, more for his harm than for his good," and say so very openly before the startled countess—he leaves her at Kilkenny under very heavy guard. He has come with ten trustworthy knights, of whom he keeps but one to escort him on his journey, and instructs John d'Erley, his cousin Stephen of Evreux, and the other seven to maintain order in his absence, to control the local vassals, gallowsbirds whom the colonial conquest has scattered over the country and whose imbroglios he is familiar with. He has collected all his knights together in the castle hall before leaving and speaks to them: "Lords, you see before you the countess whom I lead by the hand [he shows, held solidly in his own fist, this body in which flows blood bearing authority to govern the seigneury]. She is your natural lady [by birth: she is the daughter of the previous earl, the granddaughter of the former king] who invested you with your fiefs when the land was first conquered [the right of conquest has become seigneurial by the distribution and concession of feudal holdings]. She remains among you, with child [in her womb may lie the future lord, more secure than William is, since he will not rule by marriage alone, as a prince consort, but by filiation and inherited right]; until such time as God restores me, I beg you all to care for her kindly and by nature, since she is your lady . . . " Indeed, all he possesses he has through her, and we sense his anxiety at having to let her out of his sight for even a moment. Will she escape him, will he find himself empty-handed once again? Let her be closely guarded, let care be taken that no one carry her off. Let her not proceed, still so young, to God knows what secret shamelessness, fornicating so openly that he would be constrained to separate from her. One does not repudiate opulence.

O PULENCE? Here we must be careful; is it in fact opulence that we are dealing with? Let us not reason in the fashion of a modern banker. At the end of the twelfth century, money counts, and counts a great deal, as I have said. Nonetheless, wealth, and the fact that property brings in so many *livres*, *sous*, *deniers*, has infinitely less importance than power. Before taking Isabel in his arms, William Marshal was not without power. He carried a certain weight, first of all by his reputation, by his renown for military expertise: it was certain that in misfortune, in England and on the Continent, doors would open to the famous hero of the finest tournaments within memory, and that he would always find some employment within the great households. Moreover, he could henceforth count on the personal affection of several very sure friends, faithful companions of his adventures, Baldwin of Béthune first among them; lastly, he had for some time maintained his own *conroi*, a small group of intimates, young men devoted body and soul, his own squire John d'Erley first among these. Upon the accession of Richard Coeur de Lion, he is recognized as invulnerable: every man loyal to the late king protests that he will support him, that if necessary he will stand hostage for him. Even in the other camp, certain men who fear him for the support he commands and for his worldly wisdom speak in his favor to their lord; there is all he has learned about the internal dissensions of the royal house, the harm he knows and can reveal if he should speak; perhaps too are involved the old memories preserved in the Plantagenet lineage—the fact that twenty years ago he was Eleanor's champion in Poitou. In any case, Richard finds himself obliged to control his rancor and refrain from killing him, from washing the still-fresh affront in his blood, actually keeping his father's promises and, whatever his own view of the matter, providing him with a wife, making him, by this splendid gift, what William had never been except for a moment and in subaltern capacity when he served young Henry: leader of the *mesnie*, head of the household, manager.

By this gesture Richard enriches him indeed, but above all transforms him. He changes William's level in the hierarchy of social conditions; he raises him to the rank of those whose power is active and stable. For in this period the only real power belongs to married men. A man has a thousand times more worth than a woman, but he has virtually none if he does not himself possess a legitimate wife in his bed, in the heart of his own house. The still prevalent custom of forbidding most noble sons to marry aims above all at avoiding division of estates, but it has the additional advantage of reserving the attributes of true authority to only a few warriors and of subordinating all the rest to them. As a matter of fact, what advantage did bachelors have over illegitimate sons? Certain rights of ancestral inheritance. But these rights remained virtual, and almost no bachelors ever exercised them themselves, merely demanding to be maintained in a condition worthy of their rank by the old married man who headed the household—father, older brother, or else, as old men, oldest nephew. By his very condition, a bachelor was always "poor," poverty then signifying, we must not forget, not destitution but powerlessness. As an adolescent, the knight's son saw his life before him divided up into three phases by two major ceremonies, two days, two great festivities, since the community solemnized both of these rites of passage by games, merriment, and blithe extravagance. If he lived beyond his twentieth year, if he had the luck not to be cut down by one of those accidents so frequent in military apprenticeship, he was certain of enjoying the first of these days, the one which, for all wellborn sons who had not been shoved into the Church, marked the completion of "childhood" and admission into the warrior caste: this was the day of the dubbing. On it they would receive the sword, that symbol of the power to do battle, legitimately to use the force that raised them above the immature and above all commoners. The second day, though, was but a dream, and for most a chimerical one. On that day, the wedding day, a warrior crossed the decisive threshold; he entered the much narrower circle of those who really ruled. This happened to William Marshal in 1189; let us venture the phrase, *a change of class*. He had looked forward to it for a quarter of a century.

AMONG ITS signal merits, the text I am using offers that of revealing the interplay of powers on this higher level of feudal society. This society, as we know, was conceived by thinking men at the end of the twelfth century as they conceived the whole of the visible and the invisible universe: cemented by what the clerks called *caritas* and the language of the courts *amitie*, sustained by "faith," another key word evoking a combination of confidence and fidelity. On this affective relation, generating certain rights and duties, rested the coherence of a hierarchical structure consisting of superimposed layers; everything was in order, according to God's intentions, when men (no one paid any special attention to women, who constituted another genre, by definition a subject one) established at a certain level lived together in harmony, served faithfully, loyally, those who were their immediate superiors, and received suitable service from those who were their immediate inferiors. Order thus appeared based on the intermingled notions of inequality, service, and loyalty. If it established this part of society *en bloc* above all laymen, it arranged many stratifications within this ruling class, determined simultaneously by *relations of domesticity*, which assured the authority of the head of the family over all the people of his household, by *relations of consanguinity*, which subordinated younger individuals to older and the generation of the young to that of the old, by *relations of vassalage*, establishing the lord above those who had sworn homage, and lastly by *political relations* founded on the hierarchy of homage, that pyramid of which mere knights formed the base, the king the apex, and the barons the median level. These different systems of dependence often intersected, their arrangements were sometimes contradictory, but always the friendship that obliged—more or less rigorously, according to the proximity of the men involved and the quality of the relation—mutual service, counsel, and as-

132

sistance was deployed on two perpendicular axes: horizontally, it maintained peace among peers; vertically, it compelled reverence *above* oneself, benevolence *below*. Of this complex grid, William Marshal's history, in the last period of his life, affords one of the best views I know.

His marriage, raising him from that depressed, subaltern level on which celibacy confined him, fundamentally modified his position on the checkerboard of friendships and services. He already had his "people," a minor troop of servants, like that surrounding any warrior who had arrived. Now he is *patron* and when, five years later, his older brother John dies childless, this function assumes still greater scope, not only because he becomes heir to family lands—no more than a dozen manors—but because he henceforth becomes head of this family. It is incumbent upon him to feed the young, to educate them, to reward them, to house them. Just as he himself had been attached to William of Tancarville, then to Patrick of Salisbury, these boys stick to him like his shadow, boys such as John, the son of his brother Anselm, who loves him as much as he loved William and Patrick. It is to these bachelors that he is most attentive, most generous, and from them in return comes the most fervent devotion upon which he can rely. They constitute the nucleus of his household, which has suddenly assumed substance and organization: when on May 12, 1194, William embarks for Normandy, we see beside him certain heads of household services, a chamberlain, a chaplain assisted by three clerks for the records, and two ships are necessary to contain all the knights of his retinue.

As a matter of fact, numerous vassals now gather around his person. After 1189, the novelty for him, when successively visiting his wife's lands, the only man sitting in the hall, was to see the knights approaching one after the other, kneeling before him with hands pressed together, then to take these hands in his own, to raise the man who by these gestures has thereby become his own, to kiss him upon the mouth, to hear him swear his faith. He henceforth expects certain services from all those who have participated in such rites: that they be loyal, that they form his court, that they help him dispense justice, accept his arbitration, present themselves when he raises his seigneurial banner at Longueville, at Striguil, even at Kilkenny. These friendships are often of less worthy metal, but at least, forming a garland around each of the fortresses of which he is the master in his wife's name, they make him the equal of the "high knights" who once, when he would return weary, footsore, covered with glory from the great tournaments, promised him heaven and earth in order to gain his fealty. And he, who dared not permit the count of Ponthieu to treat him as an equal, today knows he is established legitimately on that very same level of power.

Once he has made the damsel Isabel his wife, he has risen one notch in the scale of dignities: from simple knight, he has raised himself to the higher grade, has entered the royal barony. The English barony is open and relatively fluid, renewed faster than on the Continent by precisely that use the king makes of heiresses. Hence it is less important for William to gain admission as their peer from the barons, many of whom are parvenus like himself, than to establish friendships among them, to gain support, to protect himself above all. For in this close milieu, jealousies, rivalries for the profits of power are acute, as brutal as and more dangerous than they appear on the lower level among the group of "young knights" who vie for a lord's generosity. To this end, William uses the children his wife regularly brings into the world: by marrying them off. His policy is that of all heads of families. These men take care that the sons of the house remain simple knights and usually seek a wife for only one, the oldest of their sons, who will succeed them. This is what William Marshal sets about doing for his firstborn—and very soon. In 1203—young William is not yet twelve—he confers with Baldwin of Béthune, the old comrade whose friendship, whose partnership in risk, has never failed him. Baldwin too had been given a wife by Richard Coeur de Lion a few years after William Marshal. He had expected the heiress of Châteauroux whom King Henry had promised him. But Richard had previously given this girl to Andŕe of Chauvigny, one of his own followers. Crowned king, he sought to make amends in order to attach to himself this aging but valuable bachelor who might be very useful to him. The wife Baldwin received in compensation made him count of Aumale. She turned out to be less fertile than the heiress of Striguil and gave him only one daughter. The latter, at least, since her father "had no child but the damsel," was a very promising match. The two old friends discussed the matter and agreed on the marriage: Baldwin would give as dowry all his lands in England and elsewhere, if the king (who was the eventual matchmaker in case of his vassal's death, and who kept a watchful eye on the entire matrimonial marketplace) would confer her. All of William's and Baldwin's friends approved the match. Good connoisseurs in horseflesh, they appreciated pedigree: both the young stallion and the filly, they agreed, came from "good father and valiant mother"; it was certain that their line would prosper. William Marshal and his friend greatly favored this alliance. They agreed that if by some mischance the child (she was less than seven) should die, young William would receive the sister God might yet permit Baldwin to procreate, for his wife was young, and that if death were to strike young William first, that the bride would be transferred to his younger brother Richard—with her dowry, of course. A betrothal of great precocity, as was then the custom: the wedding only took place eleven years later.

In truth, between the earl of Pembroke and count of Aumale the pact did not create a friendship; it proceeded from it. In order to create new friends in his neighborhood, it was his daughters whom the earl distributed. They served this purpose in great families; they were implanted in other houses in order to consolidate peace, to give birth to nephews who would love their mother's brother more than their father and who, in years to come, would hesitate to inflict too serious harm upon their cousins. William therefore applied himself to find takers for his daughters. Only one, as we have seen, remained on his hands when he died. The three older girls had been, our text says, "well employed." They were affianced to three sons of earls. William had given Matilda, the oldest, "to the best and the finest he knew," Hugh Bigod, future earl of Norfolk; the third, Sibylla, to the future earl of Derby; the second, Isabel, to Gilbert de Clare. The latter had the advantage of being earl of Hertford by his father, earl of Gloucester by his mother, as well as his future wife's cousin, and this alliance—which, we may note, defied the threats the Church hurled without much conviction against incestuous marriages—would favor the assembling of dismembered inheritances. The fourth had a less fortunate fate; when one has so many daughters, one cannot appear too choosy for the youngest ones. A good friend of the earl's, the seigneur de Briouse, who happened at the time to be in tight straits, agreed to take Eva for one of his grandsons.

Already provided on his flanks with the indispensable friendships that had grown closer during his long life of knight-errantry, but envied and hated by several clan leaders, William had thus managed, by bestowing his daughters (but at what cost? subtracting how much from the patrimony in order to constitute their dowries?), to ensure at least neutral complicities in four of the houses as powerful as his own. So much for friendship on the horizontal level. On the vertical axis, he totally dominated his wife—who had been handed over to him without any relative to defend or protect her—and their children. He held the young men and those not so young whom he fed in his own house under very close scrutiny. He counted, without being altogether sure of it, on the service of great number of enfeoffed knights. However, on this axis, he found himself in a median position, for the lands he had taken possession of by his marriage, lands that were not freeholds but feudal estates, he had had, after his wedding, to swear homage, to kneel . . . to several, but first of all to his king. To what degree, in what manner did he regard himself as a subject? And what was loyalty at this level?

Apropos this the poem has a great deal to teach us. Because of that I am consulting it now, leaving aside all it has to say about events, which is considerable and which, after 1189, constitutes almost the entire substance of the work, for since he was now a baron, the earl found himself very closely involved in politics on the highest level. But for this very reason, what the biographer reports in this regard, frequently departing from the usual narratives, has long since passed into the factual histories of England and of France too, for everything at this period links the fate of the Plantagenets to that of the Capetians. I therefore refer the reader to these histories, especially to the one that Lavisse oversaw at the beginning of this century. But I carefully retain the indications that permit a better look at how royal power was situated within the feudal system.

I N RELATION to the first two kings he served, Henry the Elder and young Henry, the *Histoire* shows William in a posture of loyal veneration. He belonged to their "family," to their house; they were like fathers to him, better still—for the bond was a much closer one—like maternal uncles. That such uncles were also kings added only a little pride to the man who, in any case, would have served them as a nephew. The affection William naturally felt for these two sovereigns, the obligations he acknowledged toward them, proceeded, in this period of his life, from the most intimate, domestic relations of dependence, compared to which the relation of subject to king appears formal, cold, without vigor, and almost without effects. As a married man, he no longer belongs to anyone else's household, he does not figure among the intimates of Richard Coeur de Lion, of John Lackland. What he owes them is of a public order. He pays what he owes, but without warmth. Of Richard the *Histoire* speaks highly but briefly: a hero of chivalry, he has energetically led Normans and English, hitherto constantly beaten, in triumph against the knights of France. On the other hand, the *Histoire* is silent about the (dubious) virtues of John Lackland, and suggests at every turn that William had no great love for him; it avoids going further; not a word is mentioned of Arthur of Brittany, whom most people believed his uncle the king had murdered with his own hands. Loyalty imposed such discretion. Yet let us note that this discretion was not incumbent upon the subject, but upon the good vassal, who had sworn, during the ceremony of homage, never to do harm to his lord's honor. For our poem makes it clear that William Marshal treated the Plantagenets as he treated the barons his peers, on the same footing, as a rival power and not a dominant one, except for the consequences of the link of vassalage.

William's biographer, whose view of this world is so profane, never makes the slightest allusion to that additional, supernatural, possibly miraculous power with which the liturgies of the coronation impregnated the royal person, disengaging that person from the feudal network, raising it to a position of intermediary between man and God. No aura around these kings; nothing distinguishes them in everyday life from the most powerful of their subjects. William, "whose heart was ever whole and pure," served them in good faith. "As lords and as kings," the text says specifically. In fact, if he served them well, it was because he had sworn homage to them. But he had sworn homage to others too, and when his obligations toward these other lords ran counter to those of the king's subject, he did not hesitate: a model of loyalty, the earl refused his service to the king in order to serve first the man of whom he was the sworn vassal, and for that reason the friend. Of all the moral codes whose rules he respected, the most constraining after the domestic was the vassalic. Also private, it always prevailed over public morality. Though the crowned king might present himself at the great festivals of Easter and Christmas as God's representative on earth, responsible for maintaining human society in those dispositions that also govern the stars, ultimately he was the last to be served.

A few months after his accession, Richard had set off for the crusades, taking with him a great part of his barony. William had not accompanied him: "he had already taken the step a man takes toward the Holy Land in order to seek God's mercy." A loyal subject, a loyal vassal, a vassal of the king . . . But because of the possessions Isabel had inherited on that island, also a vassal of the king of Ireland. That king was John, Richard's brother. John had for some time shown reluctance to receive the earl's homage: while the orphan heiress was a royal ward, he had taken her Irish lands into his own hands, treating them as his own patrimony, granting them as fiefs to his own friends. Richard would have lost his temper, would have sworn "by God's legs," and would have declared his will, whereupon John ultimately obeyed his older brother. Now that Richard was in Syria, John bestirred himself, taking all he could take in England, counting precisely on his "friends," his vassals, hence on William, using that homage which he had at first rejected, holding him by his Irish fiefs, requiring service of him. Did William serve this very present lord, capable of punishing his felonious feudatories so much more harshly than the other one who was no longer to be seen and who perhaps would never return? He was accused of as much. The *Histoire* claims that the faraway king chose not to believe those spiteful tongues upon his return, retorting that "the earl was never wicked, never false." Indeed. If William had believed himself entirely exonerated, would he—neglecting to conduct his own brother's remains to burial—have galloped so fast to meet Richard in 1194, once he learned that the sovereign had returned and was going to punish all traitors? He protested his loyalty, apparently was heard, but did not for all that break with John, whom Richard was disinheriting for having made an alliance with Philip Augustus. When Richard ordered his brother's vassals to break with John and to resume their fiefs directly from him, many consented. William did not, indeed swore he would do no such thing, resisting in the name of his double loyalty. And without fear, he asserted, because he had served in good faith, for the fief which he held from each of two lords on equal terms, not judging that, on the pretext of royalty, one prevailed over the other. Richard gave way, for he had need of all his men, of their help, of their counsel. Could he, in the name of a conception of sovereignty alien to his knights' ways of thinking, require them to betray friendships formed at the time of the oath of homage and thereby to undermine the vassalic system of values? On this system, on a similar network of friendships, was based all his power. William, because he was his vassal and his friend, served Richard faithfully in his wars against the French, at the peril of his life, like a young man storming in full armor the moats of the besieged castle of Milly. But he served within the strict limits of the feudal obligations, constrained by others of like nature: careful to do nothing that would prove harmful to John. And it was to John that he turned as to his natural lord when he learned, on April 10, 1199, on the eve of Palm Sunday, that King Richard had died of his wounds.

He is at this time in the tower of Rouen. It is evening. He is preparing to go to bed. His breeches are being removed: he immediately pulls them back on and rushes across the Seine to Notre-Dame-du-Pré, where the archbishop of Canterbury is sleeping. Tears and anger: "Prowess is dead. Who then after Richard can defend the realm? The French will rush upon us, eager to have everything, eager to take everything. Let us make haste to choose the man whom we must make our king." The archbishop inclines toward Arthur, son of Geoffrey of Brittany, the late king's younger brother.

"That would be ill done," William says to him. "Arthur is in criminal council [in fact, he was then a ward of Philip Augustus], proud and easily offended; if we raise him above us, he will cause us harm and much grief; he loves not those of the country. But consider John. My conscience and my knowledge name him to me as the proper and nearest heir of the land of his father and of his brother. To his father, as well, he is closer than is the grandson." As king, John appreciated the service rendered, restored to William what Richard Coeur de Lion had delayed giving him, all he was entitled to by inheritance and by marriage: the dignity of marshal and above all the sword of the earl of Pembroke.

Everything went smoothly until William found himself caught once again between two lords whose interests were contradictory. Indeed, he swore homage to another king, that of France, obliged to do so by family claims. John Lackland, defeated by Philip Augustus, abandoned Normandy. Could William lose Longueville and his other Norman lands? He owed it to himself to preserve them for his wife, his sons, his lineage. In May 1204, King John sent him with Robert d'Estouteville, earl of Leicester but also count of Passy-sur-Eure, on an embassy to the Capetian, whom they met at the abbey of Bec. They discussed peace with King Philip, they spoke of their Norman lands, and finally reached an agreement. William and Robert immediately each paid five hundred silver *marcs*: they would come and kneel before the king of France and from him receive their fiefs if, in a year and a day, John had not managed to reconquer the province. Hence, when eleven months later John Lackland once again sent William across the Channel for these endlessly resumed peace negotiations, he had authorized him, the *Histoire* says, in order that he not be dispossessed, to swear this homage, not wishing, he declared, that William lack means to serve him, "knowing well that the more he had, the better he would serve him."

The narrative adds, however, that John later claimed never

141

to have done such a thing, and harassed William upon his return. Preparing to cross the sea himself, he ordered William to accompany him, speaking formally before the mustered troops, demanding of him against the king of France the aid that according to the feudal custom, every vassal owes to his lord setting out to recover his inheritance. "Ah, sire, for the love of God, it would be an evil thing were I to go, since I am his sworn liege." "You hear, lords: he cannot deny what he has said. The business, as you see, reveals itself to be an ugly one. By God's teeth, I shall seek the judgment of my barons." William does not flinch, stands up, raises his hands to his forehead: "Lords, behold me, for by the faith I owe you, I shall be today an example and mirror. Listen well to the king: what he seeks to do to me he will do to each one of you, and worse still if he can." The barons look at each other; they withdraw, both from the king and from William. These two, face to face, are now surrounded only by their own men. On William's side, John d'Erley and Henry Fitzgerald, his two dearest friends who will stand beside him throughout his death agony; on the king's side, his bachelors, the young men he supports, who vie with each other to earn his love and the presents he bestows—the heiresses. The constraints that compel counsel have broken down. The public constraints of the barons with regard to their king, the private yet solid constraints of the vassals with regard to their lord when the latter summons them to argue such an accusation of felony. Only the domestic bonds have held fast, closer than the very ones that unite the sons to their father.

The bachelors support their lord's point of view and vote to confiscate the earl's fiefs, not seeing, says their spokesman, "for what reason a man might hold his land if he fails his lord in time of need." Only Baldwin of Béthune, among the barons, defends the earl. But here again it is the closest friendship that enters into play, the camaraderie of combat and perhaps much more if, reading between the lines, we suspect that there is also involved, scrupulously muffled, that love which men bear each other in the knightly companies. "Be still, it is neither for you nor for me to judge in court a knight of the earl's quality." The king does not insist, says, "Let us go to table," reflects after the meal how to take revenge, seeks someone who will defy the earl, forcing him to fight in single combat to defend his rights and perhaps defeating him . . . Finds no one who dares: weakness of the feudal power; weakness, nullity, in fact, of the royal power. Powerlessness. The sovereign can do nothing but mask his rage and put a good face on the matter. At least, invoking feudal custom—and this is his sole recourse—he obtains a guarantee that he be given as hostage the oldest son of the man he accuses, the man who has not actually betrayed him but whom he now treats nonetheless as an enemy, because, dividing his loyalty with respect to the morality of lineage, he has become, though remaining his friend, his enemy's friend as well. This is what sons are to be used for, as we have learned from the earl's own youth. And till the end, it is not on his sovereign authority, nor on the threat of confiscating William's fief for a felony judged in feudal court, it is on his vassal's sons held captive as a guarantee in his own castles, within arm's reach (that arm it was said, that had strangled Arthur of Brittany), and on other men, the earl's closest, most beloved friends, that John Lackland, king of England, will count in order to keep his subject, his sworn liege, from doing him harm.

For henceforth, beneath the appearance of friendship, lie rancor and suspicion between the king and his great baron. For this reason William feels the necessity of keeping his distance. When John returns to England on Michaelmas of the following year, the earl asks leave to visit his Irish lands: he has not yet ever seen them. Retreat to this remote country, this wild, rebellious colony, and a desire to hold fast there to what is crudest, most solid . . . The king consents, then regards himself as tricked, changes his mind, declares he has promised nothing, sends a message to Striguil. The earl is on the point of embarking. John demands William's second son as an additional hostage. "Wash your hands, go to dinner," William tells the bearer of the order. "I shall take counsel with my people and my barons" [for indeed the fate of their lord's heirs concerns the latter virtually as much as the parents]. The majority advise William to refuse, but he consents out of loyalty: "If he wills it, I shall send him all the children I have, but I shall go to Ireland, for good or ill." He leaves, and almost at once the crisis explodes apropos of a relative by marriage of the earl, whose sworn vassal he also is for certain lands: William, sire of Briouse in Normandy, but also a baron of the Welsh marches.

King John, short of cash—the pope has laid England under an interdict—requires hostages from everyone. Briouse, refusing to abandon his sons to Arthur's murderer, takes flight with his own. The earl gives him refuge, respecting the duties of kinship, of loyalty, and installs him in Kilkenny. Ordered to give him up to the king's representatives, William has him taken elsewhere, to a safe place. In pursuit of the rebellious lord, John Lackland pitches camp on William's lands, then charges him before the barons of the country gathered in Dublin. "Yes," William defends himself, "I have given refuge to my lord when, in great pain and suffering, he came to my castle. You must not take such an action ill. I had not thought of wrongdoing, for he was my friend and my sire. I had not heard any report that you were on bad terms with him. You appeared best of friends, both of you, when I left England." He declares himself ready for trial by combat. But this time as well no champion is found to stand against him. The same impotence of the sovereign, of the feudal lord, reduced to claiming further hostages. "You already have my sons and all my castles in England. If you still seek castles and fortresses, I shall give them to you, and the sons of my vassals." John deliberates with his people "in his chamber," in private, demands John d'Erley and four other knights, the most loyal of the Earl's "young knights."

William Marshal has the power to dispose of his sons as he chooses. He cannot do so with these men; they belong to him, of course, but not totally. They must give their consent, which John d'Erley does in the name of all: "I am the king's man and yours. If my lord the king requires it, I shall willingly become his hostage." Out of friendship still: "he is not a true friend who fails his lord at need." John Lackland asks more: to take the whole company escorting the earl, not as hostages, but "in pledge." This means that the knights will not surrender their bodies, but will simply promise to abandon their master if ever the latter should be at fault, and to side against him. They agree to perform this duty, which is also one of friendship. In fact, if one knight refuses, it is because the earl has indeed failed him, has caused him, he claims, "such harm that he is entitled to refuse to help him in justice, and not to pledge for him." The king distributes the five hostages among his castles in England; there he keeps them prisoner for nearly a year; indeed, one of them dies in this voluntary captivity. But the moment when John needs all his forces in order to resume war against the Welsh, he releases the survivors. This was his custom, the narrative observes severely: "he kept his men of counsel far from him until he had great need of them."

The great need arose precisely in 1213. Philip Augustus was preparing to invade England, to take it away, with the pope's consent, from the excommunicated King John. William returns from Ireland, still loyal: "he did not pay any heed to the king's cruelty." But he managed to have his two sons released, entrusted to John d'Erley, that is, to his double. Now he is very old, much too old to be useful at Bouvines, or even at Roche-aux-Moines, the two battlefields where the decisive encounter between the rival kings would be played out. There remain his sons, his natural substitutes.

The older one has slipped away. *Faute de mieux*, John Lackland takes the second with him into France to wage war, despite his father who, sensing which way the wind is blowing, tries to keep him too and claims he is "too young and tender to take to far countries." In fact, the younger boy fell ill, nearly died, and survived only by the merest chance. But his father manages to make use of his elder son, in order to conduct his policy more readily on several levels, among his many loyalties. After the defeats of 1215, the barony is in revolt. The poem's author prefers "to pass over," he says, this time of discord and disturbance, asserting that "of all this evil, nothing was done which was done by the earl." Perhaps not directly: we know nothing. It is certain, in any case, that young William, his heir and successor, immediately sided with the rebels, with another William "whom he loved like a brother," William Longsword, earl of Salisbury, King John's bastard brother. And when the following year Prince Louis, Philip Augustus's son, landed in England, the old earl did not compromise himself. It was enough for him that his elder son should be one of the first to swear homage to the invader—for the fiefs of Normandy, precisely.

A double game? Certainly. But it is no less certain that William did not betray the faith he had sworn to John Lackland. Whom he never defied. The earl never figured among the disloyal vassals whom the text calls *empris*, those who commit themselves, form a conspiracy against their lord, break with him deliberately, openly, as William of Briouse had done, as the count of Flanders and Renaud de Dammatin, vanquished at Bovines, had done against Philip Augustus. The earl agreed to furnish all the hostages, all the guarantees the lord of his fiefs required, agreed to appear before that lord's court to be judged there by his peers. If he never was so judged, this was because he was within his rights, for no champion dared risk disputing that right, which was obvious according to the dread liturgies of trial by combat. The earl entrenched himself behind the unwritten

law that obliged a wellborn man to betray none of the friendships that bound him: doing nothing, remaining with folded
arms while his various lords confronted each other, or else
letting others act for him—a member of his household such
as John d'Erley, or better still his sons, who when they were
not serving as hostages might very well, as "friends" to their
father, proudly face that father's lord. Yielding nothing, beat-
ing to windward, holding fast to his fruitful wife, William
thus remained convinced of his loyalty. Because he found
himself henceforth secure, after a long wait, and because he
wanted to risk nothing, being a prudent man, of what he
held at last; perhaps too because he was now too old, over
sixty, to venture once again into great danger, he managed
to spare himself "great shame" without renouncing his honesty. The shame of a Robert, count of Alençon, for example,
who "when King John had given him of his holdings and
kissed him on the mouth, the very same day betrayed him.
Forthwith on that day, he made the evil turn, and went over
to the king of France, did him homage and made alliance,
and put the French in his city. Shameful is the man who
willingly does a base thing."

I N OCTOBER of 1216, the majority of his barons and
knights having abandoned him and gone over to Prince
Louis, John Lackland died, almost alone, at Gloucester Castle. Speaking as every dying man should, repenting, begging
the customary pardon of all those he had harmed or offended. Mentioning the earl first of all, declaring that he had
served loyally, urging his last remaining friends to put his
son in William's care, as if the earl alone were capable of
protecting his inheritance. This child—he was nine at the
time—was in safekeeping at the castle of Devizes with the
royal treasure. Once his father had given up his soul, his few
partisans set off there to take it. William was on the lookout,
and he too set out, joining them on Malmesbury plain, and

found the boy Henry in the arms of a sergeant-royal, his "master" and virtually his nurse. "Well taught," the heir played his part perfectly, clearly uttered the formula he had learned by heart, said that he entrusted himself to God and to the earl in order that the latter, for God, in place of God, might take him in ward. The child wept, those present wept, and William himself wept tenderly. Young as he was, the new king of England had to have a sword. Consequently, had to be dubbed. Which the earl did quite smoothly: he had already had occasion to dub a king. Dressed up in royal robes hastily adjusted to his size, the little boy "was made a knight, small and fine." He was first taken to Gloucester Cathedral, where he was anointed and crowned, then to the antechamber, where he was released from the coronation vestments, which were really too heavy for him, whereupon the company passed into the hall and feasted together.

The earl hesitates to take the orphan, that is, the realm, under his tutelage, to assume the regency, old as he is. That night, in his lodgings in Gloucester Castle, he withdraws with the three men closest to him: his nephew John, Sir Ralph Musard, keeper of the castle, and John d'Erley. The first advises accepting; one must finish what one has begun: "Do it. God will help you, and from it you shall derive great honor." The second advises accepting: "You can, if it please you, make all your people rich men, and others, and even ourselves here with you." But John d'Erley can only say, "I see your body weakened by age and weariness. And the king has almost no money. I fear the worst, and great trials to come." Yet the next day, and perhaps indeed because the papal legate was cunning enough to speak of expiation, of redemption, affirming that God would remit his sins if he determined to inflict upon himself, near to death as he was, such a penitence, the earl accepts the power offered him. He uses it at once. Of the money, the "holdings" that John had so cruelly lacked at the end that everyone had abandoned him, William Marshal makes good use. He distributes all the

148

jewels gathered in the coffers at Devizes: thirty-three sapphires, fifteen diamonds—which are worth five hundred and forty *livres*—to a certain captain of the mercenaries; six rubies, seven sapphires to pay the garrisons of Devizes and Windsor; and, for the garrison of Dover now resisting the French, sixty-three lesser emeralds, thirty-three sapphires, ten new rubies, nine garnets. And no longer having enough jewels, he orders the silk garments to be sold, since he must settle these pensions called *fiefs de bourses*, must satisfy all those who serve by reason of money alone. Which permits the kingdom to survive.

He takes the same concern for his own, delivers to his elder son—who has rejoined his camp, leaving Prince Louis, since the parental bond always takes precedence over vassalic friendship—the treasure of London, that of Winchester, Durham, Canterbury, and York, and further the ward—the usufruct—of the fiefs confiscated from the rebels; enriches his nephew John, enriches John d'Erley. There remains the matter of honor. He harvests it in great armfuls. As a matter of fact, never in all his life has his war cry, his motto: *Dieu aide au Maréchal* seemed more appropriate. Heaven is on his side, which always helps the protectors of orphans. And heaven shows its favor brilliantly at Lincoln, in the summer of 1217, giving William victory.

A battle, one of those very rare trials in which two parties in disagreement, after long confrontations, determine to hand the matter over to God and His judgment, launching all their forces against each other as the champions do in single combat. The Lord God that day reveals His intentions by designating the victor and the camp where the right is to be found. For the earl, Lincoln is the Bouvines that his great age had caused him to miss. Here he takes the place of one of the kings. His function, then, is first of all, as chief officiant, to speak, to raise men's courage by successive discourses, showing evil, disrespect, and sacrilege incarnate in the adversary, repeating what is always said, down through the ages, to the frightened troops on the eve of the decisive engagement: "To protect our valor, for us, for those who love us, for our wives and our children, for the defense of our lands, in order to win the highest honor, for the peace of the Church as well, for the remission of our sins, let us bear the weight of arms . . . You are the hope of the country . . . Behold, those men are in your hand. They are ours, if your hearts serve you boldly now, without fail. If we die, God will take us to His paradise. If we defeat them, we shall have acquired lasting honor for ourselves and our descendants. They are excommunicate, and those we strike down will go straight to hell."

Yet, stiff-jointed as he is, he insists on taking part in the battle, laces up his helmet, spurs on his horse as in the past, "as light as a falcon." He advances to the front lines. He proceeds so rapidly that he grasps the bridle of the opposite leader's horse, of the man who, on the other side, also takes the king's place or the place of Prince Louis, who happens to be besieging Dover. This man is a baron, one of William's peers, the count du Perche. He will capture him. This will be his last and most glorious prize. But now, by inadvertence, a splinter slides over the surfaces of the helmet, piercing the count's eye, and he collapses and dies. It is the only death among all the knights during this fierce day's fighting, along with that of the clumsy knight who has wounded him and of a third. The king is checkmated, the match won, and the battle perfectly successful—more so than Bouvines, where the leader of the defeated army managed to get away. As in all battles, the outcome of this one suffices to reverse everything at one blow. The child-king no longer has anything to fear, and the French no longer have anything to do but decamp. But honor still obliges the earl to treat the latter nobly. As friends of long standing and as, in the past, in the evenings after the tournaments, he would treat the knights he had captured. Largesse becomes prowess. He insists on personally escorting Louis of France to the coast. A *beau geste*, regarded by many as all too *beau*: an offense. Did not interests of state make it necessary to discard, among other outmoded things, the attitudes of chivalry? Twenty years later, Henry III was to assert to Walter, the earl's third son and his successor after his deceased older brothers, that William had betrayed him: he should have kept Prince Louis and his barons in bondage. Many had thought this, some since 1205, when William had put his hands in those of Philip Augustus in order not to lose Longueville, henceforth accusing him of loving the French too much to keep his faith with John Lackland. Matthew Paris, the chronicler, expresses a common opinion when he describes the king of France, informed of the defeat at Lincoln, questioning the messengers, worrying: Is King John really dead? Is his son crowned? And is the earl still alive? Yes? "Then I fear nothing for my son." And if young William is so eager that his father's panegyric be so splendidly composed, this was doubtless an attempt to exonerate him, to wash him clean of the suspicion of disloyalty.

Was William Marshal intoxicated with power? Carried away by the joy of unexpectedly replacing, as regent of the sovereign, that indecisive man John Lackland, whom he had served so reluctantly, hating him, though without saying so too loudly? Not at all. In all honesty, William remained loyal to his own morality. Which was that of chivalry. On the second night, at Gloucester Castle, having just accepted the regency in his chamber before his three friends, his heart all at once had "sprouted": bursting into tears, he saw himself, he said, as on the high seas, lost, "no longer finding anchorage or shore." To rescue him from this anguish, John d'Erley had argued that this would be, at worst, great honor, great joy, great office, even if all the English barons were to go over to Louis of France, even if he himself had to flee to Ireland with the child Henry. And all at once William had recovered himself: "Do you know what I shall do? On my shoulders I shall bear him. From island to island . . . " This last role delighted him: he would end his days as Saint Christopher. Out of the depths of his memory there rose an image from early childhood, from the time when he used to play—even younger than this little Henry—in the arms of the then king of England. Now he was holding today's king in his arms, earthly power at the highest level it could achieve in this world. Apotheosis. For two years he could do what he would. But acting as he had never ceased to act, according to the rules of knightly honor. As a simple knight.

He had never been anything else. A younger son without possessions. Now rich and a baron, but as the guardian of his wife and of her sons. Invested with royal power, but as regent of the under-age king. Without having imagined he would accede to this degree of power. Without being trained to wield it, and without the title to do so which might come to him by blood or by the priestly liturgy. With no other virtue—and those who celebrated his virtues, speaking for him, repeating his own words, expressing what he himself believed, never sought to say anything different—than to be considered the flower of chivalry. It was to this excellence, and to this alone, that he owed his extraordinary elevation. Thanks to that great indefatigable body of his, powerful and skilled in knightly exercises; thanks to that brain apparently too small to hamper the natural bloom of his physical vigor by superfluous reasoning: few thoughts and brief, a stubborn attachment to the rough-hewn ethic of men of war whose values abide in three words: prowess, generosity, loyalty. And thanks to his longevity above all, a miracle. Have we not touched here on what is essential? In the *person* of William Marshal, in that indestructible frame, survived the twelfth century of all his early exploits, that century of tumultuous exuberance, of Lancelot, of Gawain, of the Knights of the Round Table . . . The good old days, the days gone by. He could advance calmly toward death, proud of having been the instrument of the final, the fugitive, the anachronistic triumph of honor against money, of loyalty against the state—of having borne chivalry to its fulfillment.

152

But for the last two decades, chivalry was no more, and the earl himself no more than a residual form, a kind of relic. Chivalry and William Marshal, in 1219, could no longer serve any purpose but to disguise a harsh reality by those false and consoling vanities for which each man nursed a piercing nostalgia in his heart and in the great world.

bibliography

WORKS BY GEORGES DUBY

A History of French Civilization (with Robert Mandrou). New
York: Random House, 1964.

Foundations of a New Humanism, 1280–1440. Geneva: Skira,
1966.

The Europe of the Cathedrals, 1140–1280. Geneva: Skira, 1966.

The Making of the Christian West, 980–1140. Geneva: Skira,
1967.

Rural Economy and Country Life in the Medieval West.
Columbia: University of South Carolina Press, 1968.

*The Early Growth of the European Economy: Warriors and
Peasants from the Seventh to the Twelfth Century.* Ithaca,
N.Y.: Cornell University Press, 1974.

The Three Orders: Feudal Society Imagined. Chicago: University
of Chicago Press, 1980.

The Age of the Cathedrals: Art and Society, 980–1420. Chicago:
University of Chicago Press, 1981.

*The Knight, the Lady and the Priest: The Making of Modern
Marriage in Medieval France.* New York: Pantheon Books,
1983.

WORKS ABOUT WILLIAM MARSHAL

Meyer, P., ed. *Histoire de Guillaume le Maréchal*, 3 vols.
Paris: Société de l'Histoire, 1891–1901.

Painter, Sidney. *William Marshal*. Baltimore: Johns Hopkins University Press, 1933.

Riedemann, Anton. *Lehnwesen und höfisches Leben in der altfranzösischen "Histoire de Guillaume le Maréchal." Ein Beitrag zur Kulturgeschichte Frankreichs und Englands um die Wende des 12. Jahrhundert.* Bottrop, 1938.

WORKS ABOUT THE PERIOD

Barrow, G. W. S. *Feudal Britain, The Complexion of the Medieval Kingdom: 1066–1314.* London: E. Arnold, 1956.

Beeler, J. H. *Warfare in England, 1066–1189.* Ithaca, N.Y.: Cornell University Press, 1966.

Bloch, Marc. *La Société féodale.* 2 vols. Paris, 1939–1940.

Boussard, Jacques. *Le Gouvernement de Henri II Plantagenêt.* Abbéville, 1946.

Brundage, J. A. *Richard Lion Heart: A Biography.* New York: Charles Scribner's Sons, 1974.

Contamine, Philip. *La Guerre au Moyen Age.* Paris, 1980.

Fossier, Robert. *Enfance de l'Europe, Aspects économiques et sociaux.* 2 vols. Paris, 1982.

Keen, Maurice. *Chivalry.* New Haven, Conn., and London: Yale University Press, 1984.

Le Goff, Jacques. *La Civilisation de l'Occident médiéval.* Paris/ Grenoble, 1964.

Le Patourel, J. *The Norman Empire.* Oxford, 1976.

Luchaire, Achille. *Louis VII, Philippe Auguste, Louis VIII, (1137–1228),* vol. 3, 1 of *l'Histoire de France, de Lavisse.* Paris, 1901.

Painter, Sidney. *French Chivalry: Chivalric Ideas and Practices in Medieval France.* Baltimore: Johns Hopkins University Press, 1940.

Poly, Jean-Pierre, and Eric Bournazel. *La Mutation féodale (x^e-xiie siècle).* Paris, 1980.

Poole, A. L. *From Domesday Book to Magna Carta, 1087–1216,* 2d ed. Oxford: The Clarendon Press, 1955.

ABOUT THE AUTHOR

GEORGES DUBY, one of France's greatest medieval historians, holds the chair in medieval history at the Collège de France, in Paris. He is the author of many distinguished works on French and European history, including *The Age of the Cathedrals, The Chivalrous Society, The Three Orders: Feudal Society Imagined*, and *The Knight, the Lady, and the Priest.*